THE HISTORY OF
CHRISTIANITY
AND WESTERN CIVILIZATION

2,000 YEARS *of* CHRISTIANITY'S IMPACT *on the* WORLD

By Joshua Phillips

First Printing
Copyright © 2010 Vision Forum Ministries
All Rights Reserved

"Where there is no vision, the people perish." (Proverbs 29:18)

Vision Forum Ministries
4719 Blanco Rd., San Antonio, Texas 78212
www.visionforumministries.org

Compiled by Joshua Titus Phillips

Cover Design by Austin Collins
Typography by Justin Turley

All Scripture taken from the King James Version unless otherwise noted

Printed in the United States of America

THE HISTORY OF
CHRISTIANITY
AND WESTERN CIVILIZATION

2,000 YEARS *of* CHRISTIANITY'S IMPACT *on the* WORLD

By Joshua Phillips

TABLE of CONTENTS

A CHRISTIAN PHILOSOPHY OF HISTORY, CHRISTIANITY & WESTERN CIVILIZATION

*The truth is this: The march of Providence is so slow and our desires
so impatient; the work of progress is so immense and our means
of aiding it so feeble; the life of humanity is so long, that of the
individual so brief, that we often see only the ebb of the advancing
wave and are thus discouraged. It is history that teaches us to hope.*
—*General Robert E. Lee, September 1870*

In this study guide, you will find a unique perspective on history. This
perspective presupposes that all history is providentially directed and
decreed by a sovereign God for the purpose of giving glory to His son, Jesus
Christ. It was confidence in this truth that led General Robert E. Lee to state
why "history teaches us to hope."

Without this knowledge, there is no hope in history. Without the
fundamental understanding of the sovereignty of God over all things, there

is no hope for man in a decaying world. Without hope, all man can do is live in the bondage of sin nature. If all history is providentially directed and decreed, then there are no errors, no mistakes, and everything has purpose. Though we may not see ahead of time how the pieces will come together in the infinite mind of God, everything does come together, and all within His sovereign will and providential plan for history.

This perspective also presupposes that the church of Jesus Christ is the unique object of God's love; and that, because of this, the believer has unique ownership over history. Christ specifically takes every thing and every event throughout time and uses it for His own glory and for the benefit of His children on earth. When we correctly understand and embrace this fact we become more effective leaders and disciplers for Jesus Christ. We build upon the history of the past to prepare us in the present for our future and our children's future.

THEOLOGY DICTATES YOUR VIEW OF HISTORY AND OF LIFE

This outlook on history is based on a Reformed theological and biblical perspective that presupposes the sufficiency, infallibility, and inerrancy of Scripture as it applies to all nations, dates, and events, and also presupposes the perpetuity of the church outside of Rome. This is our starting point.

THE WRONG WAY TO STUDY HISTORY

But there is also a wrong way to study history: the way most twenty-first century men and women look at the past. This is the perspective that either history is just a hopeless series of events that has, through its perpetual evolution, dropped us in our modern state today, or that history is controlled by some idea of a "fate" which moves things around in a chaotic and hopeless way without any premeditated direction. It is so important that, as Christians, we move away from both of these perspectives, since they are both unlawful and rest on a godless understanding of the universe. We must completely embrace the providential and hopeful perspective of history given to us by God.

This does not mean we can white-wash history or make the facts look rosy when they were not. This is about looking at all of life through a biblical grid. It not right to make things look perfect or Christian when they were not. This would be categorically false and deceptive as well as dangerous and irresponsible from a historical viewpoint. When we hold to a biblical view of history, we don't need to cover up the scabs throughout history because we understand that it is all used for Christ's glory. With all of history's warts, it is still God's history.

To truly understand a sovereign God, we must recognize that He will always, and has always, worked through pagans, imperfect people, hypocrites, and evil doers, for His ultimate glory. This is seen time and time again throughout the Old Testament as God used evil men or corrupt nations to ultimately bless His kingdom.

FORCE THE ANTITHESIS

Finally, we must show the inherent contrast and irreconcilability of Christ to humanism, socialism, statism, or any other "ism" that opposes the true faith. History has always involved a war of ideas, and the battles that we will see in Rome, Geneva, France, England, and Scotland over truth have many of the same objects at heart as our modern day theological battles. It must always be our goal to "force the antithesis" and to separate the cause of Christ from the confusion of secularism.

By rejecting syncretism and embracing Scripture as the sole and sure foundation of our thinking, we have a solid grid to build on and will be well on our way to becoming truly Christian historians throughout life.

GROUP DISCUSSIONS AND QUESTIONS

1. How does history teach us to hope? How should we look to history as God's blueprint for our own lives?

2. How does our theology affect history?

3. Why is understanding the sovereignty of God integral to the study of history?

4. It is not only dishonest but also unnecessary to "whitewash" history. Why is this the case?

5. What is "forcing the antithesis?"

AUDIO LECTURES AND VIDEO SERIES

Audio: Opening Dinner Message

Video: Day 1 – The Colosseum

FURTHER STUDY AND RECOMMENDED READING :

A Christian Philosophy of History, by R. J. Rushdoony

Always Ready, by Greg Bahnsen

More Than Dates and Dead People, by Stephen L. Mansfield

The Sovereignty of God, by A.W. Pink

PART I
CHRISTIANITY AND ROME

CHAPTER I

THE MEANING OF ROME

THE DEFINING LEGACY OF ROME

Rome is an appropriate place to start in a study of Christianity in Western Civilization because so much of what we see in culture today can be traced directly back from Rome and through Rome. The influence from Rome involves the many socialistic, statist, and pagan ideas and practices which were championed there in antiquity and have captured the minds and imaginations of man ever since Rome's so-called "glory days." The influence through Rome involves the ways in which Rome was used as a conduit, due to its dominant global reach as an empire, to spread other important ideas which have shaped the history of the West.

There are two primary influences on the history of Western Civilization. The first is the influence of Biblical Christianity, born in the Hebrew Republic with its emphasis on the law of God, generational faithfulness, and the duties of the Christian family to follow Jehovah in the face of a world populated by paganism. This influence matured with the fulfillment of Christ's coming in the first century and dramatically expanded due to the spread of the New Testament Church within the context of Rome's far-reaching empire.

In some respects, the story of Christianity and Western Civilization begins with the Hebrew Republic. That story, the story of the rise and fall of God's people, the giving of the law of God, the development of a familistic culture dedicated to covenant keeping and generational faithfulness, serves as a backdrop and intersects with the rise of the Roman empire.

But it is the second influence—Rome itself—with its empire, its vision of the state, its understanding of military supremacy, its views of laws, which for two thousand years have served as the backdrop for the tension between Christendom with its biblical understanding of civilization and the rise of the West within the context of Rome's pagans ideals. To understand Christianity and the rise of Western Civilization, one must understand Rome, its meaning, its sense of empire, and its vision of the state as God.

As we travel through the last two millennia of history, we see this tension between Biblical Christendom and Roman influence at every juncture. We see it with Constantine, standing in the great city of York, England, and declaring himself emperor as the Roman frontier continues to spread. We see it with Charlemagne in the city of Noyon who brings with him the synthesis of new Christian thinking and ancient Roman visions of conquest and the religious state. We see it in the medieval scholasticism of England as Roman Catholic scholars integrate the classical thinking of Greece and Rome into their theology and their worldview. We see it in the cities of Milan, Geneva, Paris, London, Scotland, and of course, in Rome itself in the architecture as syncretistic Christianity attempts to wed the theological message presented by the ancient Romans through their pillars, temples, and sanctuaries with the modern understanding of the church. We see it in Versailles as we stand in the most ornate and man-centered structure in the modern world and we note, throughout the building, sculptures, tapestries, and paintings which combine ancient Roman gods and goddesses with the sun king of the fifteenth century, Louis XIV and his heirs. And finally we see it expressed in the philosophy and messages of scholars and political thinkers over the course of many centuries who perpetually desire to identify with what they perceive to be the greatness of Rome.

Though many centuries have passed since Rome was at its zenith, men still desire to identify with the "grandeur that was Rome." What do they see in Rome's history that attracts them? They see the power of the state. In Rome, they see attempts of man to unify the world under a single banner—the idea of a "one world order." They see concepts of statist government superimposed upon a citizenry to bring about some type of godless order.

So, what then is the meaning of Rome? To the humanist, the meaning of Rome is the victory of man through the power of the state. To the Christian, the meaning of Rome is the despotism of empire, the religious tyranny of despotism, the glorification of paganism, and a warning to all times that neither man nor the state is lord. That designation is reserved for one and only one: the Lord Jesus Christ Himself.

THE STATE AS GOD

Of the many ideals advanced by the Roman empire, few were as significant as the notion of the state as God. Because there can only be one God, this ideal strikes at the heart of a critical worldview battle. In every age and time, all questions ultimately devolve to one question: By what standard? What is the standard by which man shall govern? What is the standard by which man shall rule? What laws, what principles, govern and oversee the affairs of men? What is man's highest court of appeal? In the case of Rome, the vision of the "messianic state," or the state as savior, the state as god, was preeminent in answering that question. Men, armies, futures, destinies, families—all must give way to Rome as a sovereign ruling entity.

Rome was not merely an ideal; it was a religious identity through which all of life was to be interpreted. In this sense, the deification of the emperor was a natural consequence of the understanding of the state as god. As the leaders of their nations, the Caesars were to be worshipped even as the state was worshipped. This principle of the messianic state, or the state as savior and sovereign whose goal was to bring order through redistribution of wealth and submission to the state was at the core of Roman culture. This is key to understanding the tension between the rise of Christianity and Christendom and the ever-increasing expansion of Rome.

R.J. Rushdoony observed:

> [Sovereign] was a term used to describe pagan gods, and Nero (AD 54-68) is described in an inscription as ho tou pantos kosmou kyrios, Lord of all the World. The whole issue between Rome and the early church was over lordship or sovereignty: who is the Lord, Christ or Caesar? If Caesar were lord, then Caesar had the right to tax, license, regulate, certify, accredit, and control Christ and His church. If Christ is Lord, then Caesar must be Christ's minister and obey His word (Rom. 13:1-4; Phil. 2:9-11). Paul is emphatic that every knee should bend and every tongue confess that "Jesus Christ is Lord." —R.J. Rushdoony, Sovereignty

To Rome, all religions were acceptable as long as they ultimately submitted to the worship of the state itself. Therefore, hundreds of religious sects and groups, from followers of Mithras to classical pagan antiquity, coexisted in harmony one with another under the mighty power of the religious state. All, that is, except Christianity. Christianity required exclusivity: the worship of one God and not the state and the express rejection of the worship of the state. Christianity, therefore, was at war with every aspect of Rome's foundation.

Here lies the great tension which would continue from Rome all the way to the French Revolution to the time of Adolph Hitler to the present day. With the vision of the state as god and savior, the Roman messianic state led emperors to establish the Colosseums throughout the empire to continue the pacifying the crowds and to meet their needs through the distribution of food and entertainment. The heart of the matter was really who is going to be the sovereign—God or man and the state?

In the literature of the poets, in the statements of the senators, in the words of the emperors themselves, the issue always devolved to Rome as savior. Rome as the everlasting. Rome as the messianic entity. Rome as a statist vision of God. But as all people who force themselves against God, ultimately their empire was utterly demolished. This is always the result of those who reject the One True God and embrace another divinity in His place.

GROUP DISCUSSIONS AND QUESTIONS

1. How was the Colosseum used to control the people?
2. How does this relate to Americans today? Do we have reason for concern?
3. Who were the most "popular" Roman Caesars and what was it that made them more popular?
4. The Romans were superstitious. Name two superstitions.
5. What is the heart of statism? Explain this.
6. What role did the Forum play in the community? In politics?
7. What was the Circus Maximus used for? What was the goal of this?
8. Whose house overlooked the Circus Maximus?
9. Who held the greatest chariot racing record in Rome.
10. What did Rome want to accomplish by sending troops all over the world?
11. What is a welfare state? How is this an unbiblical government system?

LECTURES AND VIDEO SERIES

Audio: Opening Dinner Message, The Colosseum, The Arch of Constantine, The Forum Part 1, Circus Maximus, The Arch of Titus, The Forum Part 2

Video: Day 1-The Colosseum, Day 1-The Circus Maximus, Day 1-Wrap-Up, Day 2-The Forum

FURTHER STUDY AND RECOMMENDED READING

The History of the Decline and Fall of the Roman Empire, by Edward Gibbon

The Two Babylons, by Alexander Hislop

The Army of the Caesars, by Michael Grant

The Fall of the Roman Empire, by Adrian Goldsworthy

The Destruction of Jerusalem, by Josephus

100 Decisive Battles from Ancient Times to the Present, by Paul K. Davis

Warfare in The Ancient World, by Sir John Hackett

Tacitus' Complete Works, by Tacitus

Rome, by Michael Grant

Rome, The Biography of a City, by Christopher Hibbert

Foundations of Social Order, by R.J. Rushdoony

The Great Christian Revolution, by Otto Scott

By What Standard, by Greg Bahnsen

The Twelve Caesars, by Suetonius

Counterfeit Miracles, by Benjamin B. Warfield

CHAPTER II

ARCHITECTURE AS WORSHIP

THE RELIGIOUS NATURE OF ARCHITECTURE

We shape architecture and then it shapes us. —*Winston Churchill*

When studying architecture, it is important to remember that architecture, like every area of life, is inherently religious. A society's religious perspective of art shapes how architecture is handled throughout that culture. It was Henry van Til who said that "culture is religion externalized." By this he meant that every aspect of the life of a society is a reflection of the true faith and priorities of that people. In few places is this as clearly seen as in the architectural philosophy and styles of the ancient Roman civilization.

In Rome, architecture was theology writ large. It was religion on bold display. And most importantly, it was a manifestation of the fundamental forms of worship that the Romans embraced. We see this in a thousand ways.

The Romans felt that architecture was so important, and so religious, that when Caesar Augustus (Octavian) began to put the Empire back together, he viewed himself as the architect of a new nation, and was called Pontifix Maximus, the highest father, combining religion, rule, and decisions of art into his role as Caesar. He endeavored to create all the externalities that communicate Empire: entertainment, the priesthood, the military, the marketplace, the baths, the roads, and the architecture which is the seamless web through all these other things. It is the architecture which brings commonality to every single one of these different elements which are going to create "Empire."

The Greeks were dedicated to marble, marble, and more marble. This is because their architectural religion was built around a philosophy of purity in the way they approached construction. In their creation, there had to be purity in every area of it in order to keep the ethical foundation of the physical foundation. So they used marble since marble represented purity to them. The downside to this approach is that, since they would not break this standard, they could not build certain architectural designs which the weight of marble could not sustain.

The Romans drew very heavily from the Greeks, but in the end created their own architectural style for building and design. They took the best from different nations, drew the strongest technological points, and then used them to create the most brilliant structures. They were not solely concerned with the "purity" of the stone; they were more interested in creating something beautiful which was also functional and durable.

This came from the philosophical perspective that there should not be tension between technical excellence and aesthetic purity. All forms of architecture had to be wed in unity. This is seen in the way that the Romans believed in grandeur, scale, and size to impress, but they also believed in pragmatism and efficiency. And they knew that the best way to do this would be a combination of concrete and bricks which would revolutionize architecture. Using their superior innovation of brick building, the Romans efficiently "beat the Greeks" because they managed to incorporate style which they knew was important, while also constructing on a grander scale and in a more efficient manner.

FIRMITAS, UTILITAS, VENUSTAS

The Romans' theology of architecture reflected a broad concept of architectural principles. The first Roman architectural philosopher was a man named Vitruvius. In his book *De Architectura*, he said that there were three specific principles which should govern every structure. These were the principles of *Firmitas, Utilitas, Venustas*: that every building or design must be solid, useful, and beautiful. As Christians we would generally agree with these points because they are very close to many principles we find within the Bible.

The Romans took these principles and used them continually throughout the empire. The Romans mastered durability in their building endeavors, as evidenced by the fact that their structures are still standing after 1700-2000 years. We also know that they achieved their utilitarian function, though it was often for a wrong or perverse purpose. But they still applied this principle. And finally, we can agree, to some extent, with the physical appeal of their monuments from an architectural standpoint. They used architectural rules which we would agree with, but they idolized the human ability to create perfection, which was their downfall.

THE DEVELOPMENT OF ROMAN ARCHITECTURE VS. CHRISTIAN ARCHITECTURE

Roman art did incorporate many Greek ideas into the Roman theology of architecture. The Golden Section, for instance, is a mathematical proportioning system that allows the designer to make judgments determining the rules of what works well within squares and rectangles of different sizes in the same way we use *pi* to determine the size of circles. The principle of Golden Section is a very useful tool and is still used today in art and design.

It is important, however, for us as Christians to remember that we may not blindly copy classical art because so much of it is derived from pagan origins. It is fine and proper for us to use principles of design such as the Golden Section, or the ideas behind *Firmitas*, *Utilitas*, and *Venustas*. But it is not lawful to base our church buildings off of the Temple of Apollo or the Temple of Saturn, for example.

Christian architecture may incorporate such concepts as proportions, scale, and natural designs, but we must stay away from the charms of classical paganism. Aesthetics are not purely subjective. We must remember that all honor must be given to God, whereas the pagans gave man the glory for all things. If we are copying the pagans, then we are robbing God of the glory owed Him.

UNDERSTANDING THE "ORDERS" OF THE ROMAN COLUMN

Perhaps the most representative piece of Roman architecture besides the arch is the column. The column symbolizes the way the Empire supported the nation and the people. Today the column has become the iconic representation of classical Rome itself.

In Rome there were three main orders, or categories, of columns: the Doric, the Ionic, and the Corinthian. Often the order of column would be determined by the capital, the design and carvings which rested at the top of the column. There were also other orders that developed from these three, such as the Tuscan order, similar to the Doric, and the Compos order, which combined the Ionic order with the Corinthian capital. But these three were the foundational orders of Roman columns.

When distinguishing between the different orders of columns, it is important to understand the elements of the column. Every column is topped by a capital. The design of the building determined the proportion of the column and therefore determined the type of capital. The capital was one of the most important parts of the column, both in representation and in structure, and it is from this name that we get our word used in context of the most important part of a nation, the Capital.

The second part of the column was the shaft. There were both fluted and non-fluted columns, but the fluting is what we often think of today when picturing a classical column. The fluting runs up and down the sides of the shaft. Finally there is the base. This is at the bottom of the column itself, and centers and maintains the weight of the column.

The columns were often placed at the front of the building, if not all around the sides, and supported the pediment. The pediment was the very top of the column where a comment would normally be left which spoke to the significance of the building.

Doric columns were some of the simplest and smallest of the Roman columns. The Doric order had a capital made of a circle, topped by a square, and had a fluted shaft with twenty sides. But the Doric order, unlike the other two orders, did not have a base. The Greeks loved the Doric order, but the Romans did not, preferring the scale of the Corinthian column instead. There are many examples of ancient Doric buildings. The most famous one is the Greek Parthenon which is in Athens.

The Ionic Order often rests on a pilaster, a decorative feature on the building. A pilaster looks like a column, but often it is not structural other than supporting the tablature above it. Other columns were always structural, supporting the architecture resting on them. Ionic columns have volutes, the swirly patterns at the top which look like ram's horns. It has been surmised that maybe this was based on sacrificial motifs. The Ionic shafts were taller than Doric shafts; and this helped to make the columns look more slender then they actually were.

The Romans liked to make their architecture a little more interesting than the Greeks. The Greeks tended to make everything flat. The Romans liked the Corinthian column because of how intricate it was. Because of its design, the Corinthian Order tends to be the prettiest of the three orders. Corinthian columns always have acanthus leaves at the top of their columns, right below a small scroll design. The acanthus was a plant that grew prevalently in Greek and in Rome, and the Romans had their own style of acanthus design. The Greeks' acanthus designs were more pointy, while the Romans' design was more rounded and smooth.

The Romans preferred the columns which were more three-dimensional in style, instead of the more flat-Greek looking columns. But the Romans liked to show off as well and would use all the orders at once. Sometimes you will see the use of all three of the common orders being used on the same building. It is quite interesting to note that the column is a dominant architectural feature seen everywhere, and today it truly represents the Roman Empire.

ROMAN ARCHES AND A CHRISTIAN PHILOSOPHY OF DESIGN

Throughout history, both art and design have been used as a way of communicate important legacies to future generations. One perfect example of this is the Roman Triumphal Arch. The arch was a majestic, useful, and architecturally sound way of honoring and lauding the great generals and armies upon their return to Rome.

When a general or emperor had scored a particularly victorious war or had done some great deed, then he would have a Triumphal Arch built for himself. This would create a historical landmark honoring him. And, as he marched through the arch upon returning to Rome, this homage to his feats would be a way of showing machismo and bravado to the commoners and citizens who observed it.

The Arch of Titus was built in commemoration of General Titus's great war in Judea and his victory at the fall of Jerusalem. Titus was a general who truly led his men, and it was said that, in the final attack on Jerusalem, he killed twelve of the garrison personally, shooting them with his bow. For this victory he was awarded a triumphal entry upon his return to Rome in 71 AD. Along with his triumphal entry came the honor of having a Triumphal Arch for him to march through. Today the Arch of Titus stands at one entrance to the Roman Forum, memorializing his victory.

The Romans rightly understood that architecture is an historic pursuit, and they therefore used it to solidify what they wanted future generations to remember about them. Architecture lends itself to such historic aims as it structures can last for decades, generations, and in the case of Rome, millenniums.

The ancients understood that there were three ways to memorialize a generation: through bodies, books, and buildings. Or to be more precise, graves that memorialize and remember our forbears, books that record events and speak to the future children, and architecture that tells of life in a three dimensional way. Many of the ancients practiced these three points of generational message.

Like the Romans, the Egyptians also buried their dead with great ceremony, markings, and monuments. They archived information throughout the kingdom through papyrus scrolls and built giant pyramids and statues commemorating their important leaders and events. The Aztecs performed many similar practices.

If we really understand our role as Christians trying to redeem the earth, then we will understand that it is our duty to take captive every part of life for Christ, even architecture. We may not leave it to the pagans; we may not accept their presuppositions of art. We must purpose with a vision to create our own memorials for future generations and to create them in a way that pleases God, is tasteful in its design, and will endure.

As Christians, when we see a building, our first thoughts should be "why is it designed this way?" We may never accept art or design purely on the grounds that "it is art" because this assumes that the worldview and theology of the designer is either neutral or inherently perfect. We must be constantly in the business of analyzing every area of life to see if it is properly portraying man's position on earth and his proper response to the Creator.

If we look at something like the Roman Arch and simply say, "Well, isn't that neat," we will miss the bigger picture. We are called instead to look at the Roman arch and say: "This is an amazing piece of artwork that was originally designed solely to glorify man above all else, therefore it is problematic since man is the creation and not the Creator. But even though they did not have a biblical view of reality, the Romans used common principles of design to create brilliant art for an unlawful purpose." This is the correct perspective to have when analyzing architecture.

Sadly, many Christians tend to just look at the art of Rome and Greece and respond by standing in stunned awe at the amazing architectural quality alone without being duly critical of the wrong religious message it conveys. Speaking of a trip that he and his wife had made to Greece, C.S. Lewis once said:

> I had some ado to prevent Joy and myself from relapsing into Paganism in Attica! At Daphni it was hard not to pray to Apollo the Healer. But somehow one didn't feel it would have been very wrong— would have only been addressing Christ sub specie Apollinius.

This is a good reflection of how so many people respond to the spell cast by ancient pagan architecture! They decide to simply allow their awe over the technological or artistic aspect to overshadow the darkness that often lies behind it.

As Christians, we are required to come to the table of historical preservation with the understanding that we are called to be nation builders who will reform every area of life—not just sit in the shadows of the pagans. This duty applies to architecture, and only when we exercise this duty will we properly understood the architectural achievements of the past and be on the right footing to create appropriate models of architecture today.

GROUP DISCUSSIONS AND QUESTIONS

1. How has modern architecture been shaped by Roman design?
2. What was the Roman arch used for? Why is this important to understanding the Roman philosophy of man?
3. Isn't architecture neutral? Explain why it is or is not.
4. What was Titus' victory? Why was it important to Rome?
5. What is noticeably absent from the depictions of spoils on Titus' arch?
6. How can books, bodies, and buildings memorialize culture?
7. Why was an arch built for Constantine?
8. What famous French arch is modeled after what Roman arch? Name both.

9. What is depicted on the Roman arches?

10. Should we blindly copy all the art of the Romans? Explain the reasons behind your answer.

LECTURES AND VIDEO SERIES

Audio: The Colosseum, The Arch of Constantine, The Forum Part 1, Circus Maximus, The Arch of Titus, The Forum Part 2

Video: Day 1-The Colosseum, Day 1-The Circus Maximus, Day 1-Wrap-Up, Day 2-The Forum

FURTHER STUDY AND RECOMMENDED READING

The History of the Decline and Fall of the Roman Empire, by Edward Gibbon

The Two Babylons, by Alexander Hislop

The Army of the Caesars, by Michael Grant

The Fall of the Roman Empire, by Adrian Goldsworthy

The Destruction of Jerusalem, by Josephus

100 Decisive Battles from Ancient Times to the Present, by Paul K. Davis

Warfare in the Ancient World, by Sir John Hackett

Tacitus' Complete Works, by Tacitus

Rome, by Michael Grant

Rome: The Biography of a City, by Christopher Hibbert

Foundations of Social Order, by R.J. Rushdoony

The Great Christian Revolution, by Otto Scott

By What Standard, by Greg Bahnsen

The Twelve Caesars, by Suetonius

Counterfeit Miracles, by Benjamin B. Warfield

Destruction of Jerusalem, by George Peter Holford

For the Temple, by G.A. Henty

A History of Architecture on the Comparative Method, by Banister Fletcher

De Architectura, by Vitruvius

CHAPTER III

THE BIRTH OF CHRISTENDOM

THE TRIUMPH OF CHRIST OVER PAGANISM

> *If Christianity had not appeared, Rome would have continued its*
> *fall and been succeeded by the warlike tribes of pagan Europe. The*
> *culture of the ancients, with their wars, human sacrifices, injustices*
> *and barbarities would have continued repetitively until today, like*
> *the incoherent histories of Asia and Africa.* —Otto Scott

There is a little plot of land on the Via Sacra which truly tells the story of Western Civilization. Standing within two hundred yards of each other sit two different buildings: the once great Temple of Saturn and the prison cell where it is believed that Paul the Apostle was detained and four epistles of the Gospel were written.

The great Temple of Saturn was the focal point of Roman worship and the centerpiece for the great Via Sacra, the "sacred walk" of the Caesars as they marched to pay homage to the gods that represented the spirit and the heart of the Roman Empire. Today the Temple of Saturn is in ruins. The gods are long "dead" and the religious priests gone. But the four epistles penned in the little cell where Paul the apostle was likely kept just across the way from that great pagan temple continue to fire the hearts of billions of people around the world. They represent the eternal truth, the one source of victory: the very Word of God, the revelation of the Lord Jesus Christ.

And here we see the beginning of the heart and soul of the triumph of the church over paganism. Paganism emerged early on during the great Babel-building time which followed the Great Flood of Noah's day. And it continued to dominate the world from the time of the Table of Nations all the way to the rise of Rome. But it will be ultimately vanquished in the Gospel of Christ.

At every point in history, we see paganism with its gods, with its vision of empire attempting to thwart the source of truth, Jesus Christ. We see the centerpiece of human history, the incarnation of the Lord Jesus Christ and his crucifixion by Rome which serves as the ultimate example of paganism, of the attempts of those false religious professors, Jews and pagans alike, to quash the truth. But Christ rose from the dead, and with His resurrection, paganism was defeated. Paganism will always attempt to stop the message of the Gospel by persecution of the church, just as it did in the early church and continues to do even now. But paganism will always be conquered in the end.

Otto Scott noted the affect that Christianity had on pagan practices as the light of the Gospel spread across Europe:

> It was Christianity alone that brought intellectual and spiritual hope, an end to human sacrifices, and the recognition of individual rights to the world. No other religion ever created a church that limited governments. That limitation enabled the free Christians of Europe to clear the land of great forests, to tame the wild beast and wild tribes, to develop better methods of agriculture and manufacture, to build cities, to create cultures that were diverse but united in a single faith, to erect the largest, richest, and most polyglot civilization the world has ever known.

THE GLORY OF THE PERSECUTED CHURCH

There wasn't any great persecution of Christians prior to 70 AD. That was because Judaism was a legal religion in the Roman Empire at that time. Rome had not made distinctions between what they thought were the "sub religions" of Judaism. Until 70 AD, they thought Christianity was just a Jewish denomination. But in 70 A.D. when Rome burned Jerusalem, Judaism as a culture-religion was over, leaving Christianity wide open for the public to view it as a new religion. With the continuation of Christianity, Rome realized that there was a new contender for the throne of "top religion." And so Christianity was made illegal.

As Christianity spread, so spread the persecution. And God worked through Rome's persecution, pagan and evil as it was. In fact, during the Apostolic days and the times of the Early Church, persecution was the primary tool He used to spread the true Gospel to all parts of the world. Without the persecution of Rome, Christians would not have been driven to the far corners of the earth where they were enabled to continue the spread of Christ's good news. Without Rome, we would not have had the tools, resources, technologies, or roads to spread the Gospel.

God used this pagan nation for His glory. He used Rome to turn the heart of the people of the nations to Him. When we understand this, the Caesars make more clear sense to us in terms of God's unfolding plan. When we understand this, we understand how God used the murder of thousands to save the souls of millions. When we understand this, we understand the epic battles of all time in their right perspective.

Rome was conscientiously polytheistic. Any faith was accepted as long as it was non-exclusive and was tolerant of all the others. Christ said He was the way, the truth, and the life, and that everyone else was wrong. Christianity taught the Sovereignty of Christ over the State. This philosophy was in direct opposition to the view of the Caesars who believed that there was no power over them. Thus began the reason for the persecution of the church. R.J. Rushdoony noted:

Technically, Rome did not believe in religious persecution. However,

because it believed in the control and regulation of all religions in
terms of its fundamental law, the health or general welfare of the
people , its policy meant the persecution of Christians.
—R.J. Rushdoony, Sovereignty

As the persecution progressed, the Christians found hiding locations and places of retreat to persevere and to continue honoring of Christ. They took refuge in the Catacombs.

The pagan custom was to cremate corpses, while Christians buried their dead. But Roman law forbade creating burial places in the city, so the Christians went underground. Beginning in the second century A.D., the Catacombs were excavated from softer volcanic rock twenty to sixty feet below the ground and covered many miles. While the initial purpose was to provide a resting place for the mortal remains of the dead, the Catacombs also provided a safe haven of protection from the Roman state. The dark and maze-like passageways sheltered meetings and gatherings for the persecuted.

While the Catacombs remind us of the times of persecution, they also remind us of the hope of the resurrection of the dead. And they should remind us of the ingenuity of the New Testament Church to be able to survive in the midst of horrific circumstances.

A true Christian lays everything down for his faith, puts everything on the line for Christ, and understands that it may mean death. This was a time so dangerous and dark that Christians never knew if they would see their friends again. The heart and soul of the meetings in the Catacombs was that to be a Christian meant to be in constant risk of death and to be willing to do anything to spread the truth of Christ.

The first few centuries in Rome birthed the statement, "The blood of the martyrs is the seed of the church." For every Christian that was martyred, dozens came to Christ. In the end, Christianity took over and the polytheistic, man-centered ideals of Rome were put down.

Rome, in persecuting the early church, was trying to preserve its
law-order; the emperors clearly saw the issue: Christ or Caesar.

*Their moral and religious premise was false, but their civil
intelligence was sound: either the pagan empire or the church had
to die. They failed to see that the empire was already dying, and
that the death of Christians would not save Rome's failing life. It
was Constantine's grasp of this fact that led to the recognition of
Christianity.* —R.J. Rushdoony, The Institutes of Biblical Law

THE DISSEMINATION OF THE GOSPEL

It is one of the great ironies of history and testimonies to the providence of
God that it was the very enemies of the Gospel who used their technology
and their vision of empire to give Christ the greatest victory. That victory
came as the testimony of Scripture, the message of the apostles and their
disciples, and Gospel evangelism was spread to the four corners of the earth
through the Roman road system and the expansionistic vision of global
dominion espoused by the Roman Empire.

We see how the Gospel had reached all the way up, into, and throughout
the leadership of Rome, permeating its military and every aspect of the
Roman Empire. Note that the Scripture speaks of the Christians within
"Caesar's household" in Philippians 4:22. This was the penetrating nature of
Christianity. But it was the technological tools and the vision of the Roman
Empire which were used of God to get that Gospel message out far and wide.

One of the ways that Rome was used by God to promote His ultimate
plan and purpose was through the Roman roads, and specifically through
the Appian Way. The Roman Empire was based on military might. It was
based on the fact that Rome had military prowess above all nations. With this
prowess they continued to expand, and to expand they had to build roads.
And the roads they built began to connect the world and spread the Gospel
to all the nations.

It was the Appian Way which allowed merchants, soldiers, as well
as evangelists to travel deep into Europe to reach distant pagan tribes
and nations. It was the spread of the military and the establishment of
households in distant lands which would one day be known as France,

Scotland, England, and Germany which first brought the message of the Gospel to families around the European continent and to the British Isles.

The Appian Way was the road through which the Gospel was disseminated throughout the world during the trials of the early church. For every stone added to the road by a Roman engineer, there were more places being added to the network and structure connecting the growing "underground" community of Christians. When Rome was trying to build its empire, it was actually building Christ's kingdom. If we understand a sovereign God, we realize that God is always in the business of working through pagans to show His perfect will.

Part of the technical importance of the Roman road was that it was flat enough and smooth enough to transport any type of supplies needed by the army. So there was not as much risk to the equipment which was being transported as there had been in the past or as there was in other parts of the world. Unlike most roads of its day, the Appian Way could be refurbished and had road gangs who would maintain the roads. Because almost all the roads connected to the Appian Way, and because it was the primary road leading to Rome, this idiom was handed down to us: "All roads lead to Rome."

Especially important to the Roman army were roads leading to military cities and coastal cities with ports. The reason why the Roman armies built roads everywhere they went is because they understood they were not just fighting immediate wars. They knew that whatever they did had to last for generations of military maneuvers and supply trains. Their roads were so well built that many of them have been preserved in good condition to this day.

The roads were the means by which Rome transported its armies to foreign battle fronts and they conquered the world. However, roads work both ways, and eventually the barbarians who invaded Rome came using the very roads that Rome had built. In the end, all roads did indeed lead to Rome.

Ultimately the Appian Way, the other road structures, and the Romans themselves were the most important ways the Gospel grew throughout Europe. As more and more roads were built and more and more military families and their households were shipped to the far corners of the earth, they became the means to spread the good news of Christ to people of all classes all over Rome—and ultimately the world.

GROUP DISCUSSIONS AND QUESTIONS

1. What is the name of the Christian Caesar? What distinguished him?
2. We need to know about the Caesars, particularly the twelve, because they overlap the life of the early church. Make a timeline of the first twelve Caesars and include significant biblical events.
3. What is the original Roman definition of *pietas*, or pious, and how has the meaning changed?
4. What is the Via Sacra?
5. With Paul's cell right on the edge of the Forum, what might he have seen through the cell bars?
6. No empire can withstand what force?
7. How did Roman roads carry the Gospel?
8. How were the Roman roads a multigenerational project?
9. What does the idiom "All roads lead to Rome" mean?
10. What slave revolt has made the Appian Way famous?

LECTURES AND VIDEO SERIES

Audio: Outside the Catacombs, Catacombs, The Appian Way Part 1, The Appian Way Part 2

Video: Day 1-The Appian Way, Day 2 - The Catacombs, Day 2-Wrap-Up

FURTHER STUDY AND RECOMMENDED READING

Warfare in The Ancient World, by Sir John Hackett

Rome: The Biography of a City, by Christopher Hibbert

The Twelve Caesars, by Suetonius

CHAPTER IV

THE ROMANIZATION OF CHRIST'S CHURCH

EMPIRE AS IDOLATRY

The fourteenth-century Renaissance humanist Petrarch posed this question, "What then is all history but the praise of Rome?" Petrarch, called the father of humanism, believed that everything preceding the era in which he lived was full of ignorance and therefore coined the term, "The Dark Ages." His question regarding Rome's centrality to all of history is the ultimate manifestation of the concept of Empire as idolatry. The hubris here is palpable.

Just after the destruction of the Temple in Jerusalem in 70 AD by soon-to-be Emperor Titus, the Colosseum was constructed in Rome. And it was constructed using the profits captured at the fall of the Temple. The symbol of worship to the Hebrew God was destroyed and the centerpiece of Roman statism was created. This encapsulates the practice and philosophy of Rome: destroy all history which does not praise Rome and Rome's gods.

The Colosseum became the center of the welfare state where the people were lulled into pacifism by entertainment and government handouts. Extraordinary events drew the mobs into the arena to watch plays based on mythology, animal hunts, executions, gladiatorial contests between men and animals as blood carnage and men against men, battle re-enactments, and even mock sea battles with full-size ships.

The heart of statism is the control of the citizens, and what better way to control the citizens than to give them what they want: games, food, and as they lusted for more and more, blood. Idolatry of the Empire created a blood lust. Human sacrifice feeds the Empire since the only purpose for the citizen is to serve the state.

This was the living picture of an idolatrous vision of empire. A vision of empire that said everything, "all history", was to be used for the praise and lauding of Rome. This was a vision of the savior-state, a man-centered, socialistic, and hedonistic state and nation where the goal was controlling the people, not leading the people. The activities in the Colosseum met the immediate wants of the people, even as they became more base and depraved. Through the distribution of food and entertainment, the government grew bigger and so did their sin. In his book *Pompeii*, Ian Andrews writes:

> We often ask, 'Why did the Romans, who paid so much attention to public religion, enjoy such a terrible slaughter at the amphitheatre?' Part of the reason, perhaps, lies in the fact that the Roman gods and goddesses were not thought to be concerned about whether people did good or evil. If the right sacrifice was made at the right time, the gods would keep their share of the bargain and make things turn out as wanted. —Ian Andrews, Pompeii

As Rome tried to please the people more and more, its deeds became darker and darker. The so-called grandeur of Rome was simply a bloody sham. Otto Scott states:

> That "grandeur" was based on slavery, used torture as an

*instrument of the courts, and human sacrifice as part of religion
and politics. Such sacrifices, said Acton, "were the turning point at
which paganism passed from morality to wickedness."*

In Rome, blood sacrifice became common. Just as the gladiatorial combat
had fueled the populace's lust for excitement, so blood sacrifice fueled the
populace's superstitions. Scott notes:

*Euripides described the Greek sacrifice of Iphigenia; Herodotus
described human sacrifices in Egypt, Plato spoke of human
sacrifices as "a common custom." In Rome sacrifices "for magical
purposes" were outlawed from 95 B.C., but human sacrifices for
religious and political reasons were conducted in public for as long
as Rome was pagan.*

*In 63 B.C. Cataline and his accomplices sacrificed a boy and
ate his bloody flesh to ratify their oath of conspiracy. Julius Caesar
sacrificed mutineers in the name of Mars; Augustus, Nero, Caligula,
Commodus, Marcus Aurelius—indeed, all the Roman emperors
until Constantine—ordered human sacrifices.*

*Julian the Apostate, who tried to restore paganism and persecuted
Christians, "filled his palace at Antioch with the corpses of human victims
. . . After his death the body of a woman was found hanging by her hair in
a temple at Carrae. He had inspected her entrails to divine the issue of his
campaign. . . .*

Is this the grandeur and glory that people look to in Rome? No, this is
because this bloody aspect of the Romans is often hidden from sight while
the "glorious deeds" are remembered. Today, people still tend to look at the
idolatrous empire of Rome the way that Petrarch did. But they don't really
understand what that means.

What Petrach was saying was that there has never been nor will be
any state as great as Rome. Rome was perfect, thus man can be perfect.
Everything that Rome did must go unquestioned. Whether it was blood
sacrifice or victorious parades, Rome is, by definition, greatness. Everything
lives solely to glory in the man-centered statism that Rome personified.

Our will as humanistic men is the law, and we are not under anything other than our own wills. We are sovereign; we are law. Rushdoony explained the essential link between law and sovereignty this way:

> *Law is the expression of the will of the sovereign power, and nothing and no man can prevail against the sovereign. If man or the state is sovereign, than the sovereign will prevails, and the sovereign, as the source of law, cannot be bound by any law. If, however, God is the true sovereign over all things, all things are subject to Him, under His law-word, and shall be judged by Him. The importance of the Last Judgment has receded in theology and life as Biblical law has been neglected.* —R.J. Rushdoony, Sovereignty

Rome was trying to show that man was law and man was sovereign, but man is not sovereign and therefore man cannot be law. There is never room for two gods; there can only be one. So when Rome continued to try to prove that it could be god, it was crushed by the One True God.

Today, the Colosseum still stands as an iconic symbol of the Empire of Rome, but it stands in crumbled pieces, destroyed by stone robbers and by the elements of creation itself. But the work of the risen Jesus Christ proceeds and prevails. The construction of the Colosseum may have been, in some way, an attempt to replace the Temple of Jerusalem, and by it to symbolize the standing of Rome's god over the true God revealed in Holy Scripture. But today the Rome that once was is no more, and we know that the gates of hell cannot prevail against the church of Jesus Christ.

ARCHITECTURE AND THE ROMANIZATION OF CHRISTIANITY

As pagan Rome began to experience its demise and as the Roman emperors began to embrace elements and forms of Christianity, there were huge implications for how architecture was viewed. A classic example is found within the Pantheon itself. The Pantheon, which is considered to this day one of the greatest architectural forms in all of Italy, was established as the center of the cult worship of many gods in Rome. For centuries, Christians would not use the building for this reason, and the Pantheon fell into disrepair. But later on, with the syncretism of the Roman Empire with the Roman Catholic model of Christianity, it was no longer deemed offensive to build upon the high places of Rome. Because many of the gods and goddesses of ancient Rome were being given new names by Christians and incorporated into their practices in the form of saints and rituals and holy days, objections to the use of the buildings of Rome's pagan past quickly disappeared. This marked the substantial change from the time period of the early church to the new age of "The Roman Church." This represented a prolific season in the Romanization of Christianity.

During the time period of the early church, Christians had stayed away from the forms and the structures of Rome. The temples, the columns and the buildings—all of these structures were directly associated with paganism, and they were an expression of the pagan belief system. So as the Roman church began to take on forms of paganism, the very forms of the buildings they erected, both in Rome and throughout Europe, incorporated the theological ideals of Roman paganism into their architectural designs. The result was a Romanized Christianity.

So, where for the early Christian, there had always been a great distinction between their forms and the forms of Rome, the new church began to appear more and more pagan in its theology and architecture. For example, Romans viewed the temple as the centerpiece of worship; Romanized Christians began to do the same with their new cathedrals. For the Early Church, the building was not the issue. This is why Christians could worship in glens, under the ground in catacombs, and in houses, as recorded in the book of Acts. It was the gathering of the saints, not the location, that mattered. This was not merely a decision made out of exigency of circumstances. It was a philosophical distinction between the Early Church and the Roman Empire, a distinction that became blurred when Christians began to syncretize their practices with Roman ideals.

As the Roman Empire began to syncretize with Christianity and individuals like Constantine began to claim the throne of Rome as a vehicle for enforcing his own understanding of Christianity, the old icons and buildings and structures which were once part of paganism were now adopted and modified to be used by Christianity. This was the great move toward the Romanization of Christianity and became a tension point which exists to the present day—between a religion which is set apart from the ancient classical forms and philosophies contrasted with one which is synthesized with it.

There was also a marked contrast with how Romans and Christians disposed of their dead. Normally, the Romans burned their dead. Early Christians buried their dead instead. Consequently, they looked for permanent places to inter their deceased loves ones and often did so in the miles and miles of underground passage ways and tunnels that became known as the Catacombs of Rome. This was just one more difference between the Romans and their understanding of life, death, and reality, and the Christian perspective.

THE MOVEMENT TO ROMANIZE MAN'S MIND

In the ancient classical world, man was the measure of all things. And the mind of man, his autonomous reason, was the one source of revelation to know truth. It was the highest court of appeal. So for Aristotle and Plato, for Socrates, for Romans and Greeks alike, the ultimate quest for the philosopher was to know truth through observation and through reason, but always apart from God or His direct revelation through Scripture. For this reason, philosophy dominated the culture in Greece as well as in Rome. It was this exaltation of the mind of man and philosophy which became the great tension point in the development of Christianity and Western Civilization.

The Apostle Paul himself warned Christians not to be ensnared by the man-centered philosophies of the pagans in his letter to the Colossians:

> *Beware lest any man spoil you through philosophy and vain deceit,*
> *after the tradition of men, after the rudiments of the world, and not*
> *after Christ. —Colossians 2:8*

Paul wrote this to prepare the church for the ongoing struggle between the true faith and the false philosophies of men, and his foresight to address this issue through the Holy Spirit's leading was well-placed. From the time of the Early Church all the way up to the present day, there has been a great debate between Christianity and paganism, a great antithesis between Jerusalem and Athens, as the church father Tertullian recognized:

> *What indeed has Athens to do with Jerusalem? What has the Academy to do with the Church? What have heretics to do with Christians? Our instruction comes from the porch of Solomon, who had himself taught that the Lord should be sought in simplicity of heart. Away with all attempts to produce a Stoic, Platonic, and dialectic Christianity!*

Tertullian correctly identified the tension between biblical authority of the Scripture as the source of understanding and truth, versus the world, the gods of classical antiquity, which ultimately pointed to the mind of man.

In the nearly two-thousand-year struggle between Christianity and Rome, the root issue at stake has always been: By what standard? By what standard shall civilizations rule; by what standard shall they govern; by what standard shall decisions be made? For Augustine of Hippo, that standard was the Word of God. He pointed men back to the Scriptures, the ultimate and final court of appeal. But centuries later, Thomas Aquinas would revive the ancient Greek philosophy and incorporate it into the theology of Roman Catholicism with what has now been called "medieval scholasticism."

For the medieval scholastic mind, the world was divided into two different corners. There was the sacred and there was the secular. They believed that the Bible spoke to things which were sacred. These were matters which were primarily addressed by the church. However, the mind was left to address the world of all things secular. This dualistic dichotomy brought with it philosophies like Gnosticism, an ancient heresy which said that material things are wrong, while spiritual things are good. Thus dualism and a dichotomous approach to reasoning dominated the medieval mind. At the heart of Aquinas' error was a misunderstanding of the fall of man.

Thomas Aquinas believed that at the time of the Fall, man was affected physically and affected spiritually, but his mind was not fundamentally affected by sin. Thus, man, unaided by the Holy Spirit and unaided by Christ's sovereign grace, could determine what was right and wrong and could understand spiritual matters through "right reasoning" apart from the revelation of the Bible or through the working of the Holy Spirit. This idea that man's reason was sufficient to come to know truth independent of revelation represents the fundamental tension between Roman Catholicism and the classical world on one hand, and the world of the Reformers and Biblical Christianity on the other.

Just as Thomas Aquinas had sought to blend classical thought with Christianity and had said that man can use his reason to understand most things, so the Renaissance came around and said that if we could understand some things in life without the Bible, then why did we need the Bible at all? We didn't need the Bible to understand anything! This brings us back to the ancient perspective that the Romans embraced: man's mind is autonomous and needs no higher authority to separate good from evil.

But in the sixteenth century, the Reformation came, and with it came the "Solas of the Reformation." These were statements such as *Sola Scriptura*, the Scripture alone, and *Solus Christus*, through Christ alone, which helped to turn the church back to the root of all wisdom, the Scriptures, to discover how to truly identify the right and wrong way to understand reality. This was a radical shift for the better from the former Romanistic view of church and life.

GROUP DISCUSSIONS AND QUESTIONS

1. Who was Petrarch? What was his influence?

2. Why did he coin the term "The Dark Ages?"

3. Petrarch said, "What then is all history but the praise of Rome?" This became the theme of the Renaissance. What is the problem with this statement?

4. How did the Romanization of Christianity affect architecture?

5. Does it matter if we use architectural elements that have their roots in paganism? Why?

6. Why don't Christians burn their dead like the pagans?

7. How did Constantine affect the romanization of the church?

8. What did Tertullian mean when he asked what the children of Jerusalem had to do with the schools of Athens?

9. What do we mean when we ask, "By what standard?" Why must we ask this?

10. What was Aquinas' error?

11. What did the Fall affect man and how can you prove this through Scripture?

LECTURES AND VIDEO SERIES

Audio: The Pantheon, Pompeii: Suetonius and Tacitus, A Look at Julius Caesar and Octavian Augustus

Video: Day 2-The Catacombs, Day 2-The Pantheon, Day 2-Wrap-Up

FURTHER STUDY AND RECOMMENDED READING

The Language of Architecture, by John Summerson

Roman Catholicism, by Lorraine Boettner

Counterfeit Miracles, by Benjamin B. Warfield

Foundations of Social Order, by R.J. Rushdoony

The Twelve Caesars, by Suetonius

The Caesars, by Tacitus

For the Temple, by G.A. Henty

Beric the Briton, by G.A. Henty

Christians and the Fall of Rome, by Edward Gibbon

Foundations of Social Order, by R.J. Rushdoony

CHAPTER V

A PROFILE IN THE JUDGMENT OF GOD

GOD'S PROVIDENTIAL HAND IN HISTORY

As for such as turn aside unto their crooked ways, the LORD shall lead them forth with the workers of iniquity: but peace shall be upon Israel. —Psalm 125:5

History is linear. It has a beginning and an end. It is not cyclical, as the Greeks taught. Cycles don't start anywhere, don't go anywhere, and have no purpose or meaning. The common statement "what goes around comes around" comes from this false Greek philosophy. However, a true biblical philosophy of history shows us the annals of time as a meaningful train of events, determined by a sovereign Creator, with a starting point and an appointed goal. History is truly "His story." It is the story of God's hand in the life of nations. There would be no history without the God of the Bible, without Jesus Christ.

In order to understand history, we must interpret events through the grid of Scripture and through the eyes of the Creator, who is the author of history. When we seek to understand history in light of the basic principles, laws, and truths of Scripture, we see the meaning and purpose behind events throughout time. This is the antithesis of the humanists' perspective that we are stuck in a vicious cycle which continues to turn as we continue to evolve in circles.

One principle we find in Scripture is that obedience brings blessing while disobedience brings judgment. This is a biblical principle which many nations throughout history have recognized in their moral codes. And this is seen over and over again throughout the Bible.

> *Now therefore, if ye will obey my voice indeed, and keep my covenant, then ye shall be a peculiar treasure unto me above all people: for all the earth is mine. —Exodus 19:5*

> *Yet they obeyed not, nor inclined their ear, but walked every one in the imagination of their evil heart: therefore I will bring upon them all the words of this covenant, which I commanded them to do: but they did them not. —Jeremiah 11:8*

> *O Lord, You are my God; I will exalt you and praise your name, for in perfect faithfulness you have done marvelous things, things planned long ago. You have made the city a heap of rubble, the fortified town a ruin, the foreigners' stronghold a city not more; it will never be rebuilt. Therefore strong people will honor you; cities of ruthless nations will revere you. —Isaiah 25:1-3*

This last passage in Isaiah speaks to the awesome display of God's power in history and to the carrying out of His eternal plans in perfect faithfulness to His words. A perfect example of this is the story of Pompeii. Pompeii was a city that was bathed in sin and immorality of the worst type—the very types of sin that beset our own nation today. Because of this, Pompeii was wiped out in an instant.

The present opinion held by so many people says that God makes all the good things in the world happen while the devil makes all the bad things happen. What a horrible world it would be to live in if this were true! What type of god is a god who is only partially in control and who has no control over the hardest things in life? But this view of reality is false. The Scriptures tell us that our God controls everything that happens and has a purpose and a plan for everything in life, whether it is good or bad, even the destruction of cities. In Amos 3:6, the prophet states, "If there is calamity in a city, will not the LORD have done it?" (NKJV).

God even had a plan for the destruction of Pompeii. The eruption of Mount Vesuvius was a display of God's awesome power, carrying out His eternal plans in perfect faithfulness to His Word. He promised devastation and judgment for perversion without repentance. And he promised that the ruthless nations will, in the end, be forced to their knees in reverence for Him.

In a moment, Pompeii was destroyed, but what was left was a literal photo negative for us to look at today. Their judgment was so catastrophic that it left a picture for us, eighteen centuries later. In Pompeii, we can see, as nowhere else in the world, the consequence of sin, rebellion, and perversion.

DAILY LIFE BEFORE JUDGMENT

Arise, go to Nineveh, that great city, and cry against it; for their wickedness is come up before me. —Jonah 1:2

Pompeii was a city that stood along the west coast of modern Italy. It was the San Francisco, the Las Vegas, the New Orleans of its day. Pompeii was destroyed and completely buried during the catastrophic eruption of Mount Vesuvius. Buried underneath fifteen to twenty feet of ash and debris, it took more than 1600 years for it to be rediscovered. Even then, it was only recently excavated towards the end of the nineteenth century. Today it rests a warning to all people of what will happen to all sinful nations.

In the nineteenth and twentieth centuries, archeologists and researchers were able to come into Pompeii and begin a restoration process that has continued to the present day. As the archeologists began to dig, they found cavities in the ground which were in the shapes of contorted humans. One man, Giuseppe Fiorelli, realized that these were cavities left by the decomposed bodies of people who were buried in the solidified ash from Mount Vesuvius. Fiorelli came up with the technique of pouring plaster into the cavities and was thus able to produce perfect recreations of the last moments of the people of Pompeii.

The results which survive to this day are very detailed but eerie forms of the people of Pompeii who failed to escape. Many of the plaster casts show them in their last moment of life, with clear expressions of terror.

The story of Pompeii is the story of God's sovereign hand bringing to an end a culture which was completely caught up in depravity. Pompeii was a technologically modern city. It had running water, a sewage system, public baths, a gymnasium, a stadium, and temples of worship. But it had the depravities of a modern city as well. And the sins of Pompeii are literally frozen in time for us to look at today.

Is the story of Pompeii a story of a town that was wiped out by accident? No. God's destruction came upon Pompeii the same way it came upon Sodom and Gomorrah. But there is another important part of the story from the destruction of Pompeii.

The people of Pompeii had been given a warning just as Nineveh had been sent a warning through Jonah. On February 5, 62 AD, Pompeii was shaken by an earthquake which made the very knees of the city to knock and which did enormous damage to the city itself. The people of Pompeii had been used to minor earthquakes in the region for centuries, but the earthquake of 62 AD was a very different sort of disaster. By today's standards the earthquake would be registered over 7.5 on the Richter Scale, while the recent earthquake in Haiti was only a 7.0. In fact, historians have stated that much of the actual destruction to the buildings and monuments we see today in Pompeii was from the earthquake that predated the eruption of Mount Vesuvius in 79 AD. One writer says:

> Chaos followed the earthquake. Fires, caused by oil lamps that

*had fallen during the quake, added to the panic. Nearby cities of
Herculaneum and Nuceria were also affected. Temples, houses,
bridges, and roads were destroyed. It is believed that almost all
buildings in the city of Pompeii were affected. In the days after
the earthquake, anarchy ruled the city, where theft and starvation
plagued the survivors.*

Many people left the city after the first earthquake. It is unknown how
many people actually did leave, but a considerable number did indeed move
away from the devastation and on to other cities within the Roman Empire.
Some continued to live in Pompeii and tried to rebuild, but sadly they did
not forsake their evil ways. But this warning was rejected, and because of it,
Pompeii would be destroyed.

That photo negative which remains in the place where Pompeii once
stood gives us an intimate look into the daily life of one of the greatest
tourist attractions in all of the Roman Empire. Pompeii was an affluent
coastal city belonging to the Romans which stood about five miles from
Mount Vesuvius. It was populated by upper-class citizens, scholars, and
the well-to-do, but it also contained some of the most perverse forms of
decadence known to Rome.

THE REASONS FOR THE JUDGMENT

*Because they have forsaken me, and have burned incense unto other
gods, that they might provoke me to anger with all the works of
their hands; therefore my wrath shall be kindled against this place,
and shall not be quenched. —2 Kings 22:17*

The perversity and immorality that reigned in Pompeii was to such an extent
that at some point, after the explosion of Mount Vesuvius over Pompeii,
a Jew who lived in the outskirts of Pompeii wrote on a stone the words
"Sodom and Gomorrah," drawing the symbolism between Pompeii and the
cities which were destroyed by God for their immoral and perverse ways.
Just as God's destruction of Sodom and Gomorrah was a direct punishment

from God, so the destruction of Pompeii was a direct judgment of God upon a city practicing some of the worst perversities imaginable.

Today when we look at the ash-frozen picture of Pompeii, we see a city laid out with great planning and thoughtful design; streets with beautiful homes decorated by ornate tile mosaics; fountains both decorative and functional, several of which have been restored to use today. We see the business section with store fronts and a first century version of a fast food restaurant. We see family life in the form of an expectant mother and a pet dog both frozen in their last positions before death, as well as family shrines and altars to pagan gods, built into the walls of so many houses.

Pompeii, a coastal town, a city to which the rich would go for vacation, was a city that had two sides to it. On the one hand it was a technologically advanced, well-governed, industrious town in which thousands of people lived. On the other hand it was one of the most immoral and disgustingly perverse towns of ancient Rome.

We see the prevalence of false worship on a city scale as well in the Temple to Jupiter which looms above the city on the highest point and in the Colosseum, replicating that same building in Rome. And then, there are the darkest images imaginable. Places and pictures of the most deplorable, reprobate activities practiced by the most perverse and rebellious.

In Pompeii, many of the practices common in the Roman Empire were carried to an extreme. Abortion and infanticide were practiced. Sexual debauchery became common. In certain restricted areas of Pompeii, the walls of the houses are covered with pornographic paintings and statuary so foul that the "liberated" tourists of today are not allowed to see it without special permission.

Pompeii's Colosseum hosted games filled with brutal killings. Prostitution was a thriving business in the city. Nudity was common in large areas of the city. The town was even run on a socialistic premise: that the city owned large portions of land and property and "rented" it out to private citizens. All this and many other things too horrible to state. This is what led to the destruction of Pompeii.

And so the photo negative we see throughout Pompeii is encased in death. Death came everywhere and to everything. E.T. Salmon observes:

> *Pompeii undoubtedly played only a minor role in the main course of Roman history, but by emerging from its ashes it has illuminated the social aspects of that history. The buildings of Pompeii and the innumerable scribblings on their walls present an authentic picture of everyday life in a town of the Roman Empire. . . .* —Encyclopedia International *(1966 edition)*

On August 24, 79 A.D., just nine years after the fall of the Temple in Jerusalem, Mount Vesuvius erupted. Ash clouds enveloped the sky, falling on the city of Pompeii with almost no warning. Volcanic magma swept from the mountain into the coastal tourist city. The result was comprehensive. Total destruction and death reigned everywhere. Why did this happen? Because of sin. Why? Because of God's supreme judgment and sovereign will. Why? To serve as God's warning for those who came after.

The destruction of Pompeii took place over the course of twenty-four hours, but the initial destruction was completed within instants. The morning of the 24th began like any other day for the citizens of Pompeii. But they would rapidly discover that it was a different day from any they had ever had before. When Pompeii erupted, it shot boiling rock high into the air along with poisonous gasses from deep within the belly of Mount Vesuvius. As the magma began to cool in the air, it formed pumice stones. Along with the falling pumice came larger rocks and dense ash.

As the people of Pompeii began to realize the danger confronting them, they began to try to flee. But as more and more ash and rubble began to fall on the city, it was obvious that death was coming by asphyxiation, with the rocks and pumice stones only adding to the carnage. Most estimates say that by the middle of the first day, Mount Vesuvius had already dropped more than a hundred million tons of pumice and ash on Pompeii.

Gaius Plinius Caecilius Secundus (61 A.D. - 112 A.D.), better known as Pliny the Younger, was a lawyer, writer, and magistrate in Ancient Rome. His uncle, Pliny the Elder, admiral of the Roman fleet, had helped raise and educate him. Both Pliny and his uncle would witness the eruption of Mount Vesuvius, but his uncle would die while leading a rescue mission to save some of the inhabitants of Pompeii. At the time, the younger Pliny was only eighteen. A few years later, he would record the destruction of Pompeii in a letter to Cornelius Tacitus. Pliny wrote:

> My uncle was stationed at Misenum, in active command of the fleet. On August 24, in the early afternoon, my mother drew his attention to a cloud of unusual size and appearance. He had been out in the sun, had taken a cold bath, and lunched while lying down, and was then working at his books. He called for his shoes and climbed up to a place which would give him the best view of the phenomenon. It was not clear at that distance from which mountain the cloud was rising (it was afterwards known to be Vesuvius); its general appearance can best be expressed as being like an umbrella pine, for it rose to a great height on a sort of trunk and then split off into branches, I imagine because it was thrust upwards by the first blast and then left unsupported as the pressure subsided, or else it was borne down by its own weight so that it spread out and gradually dispersed. In places it looked white, elsewhere blotched and dirty, according to the amount of soil and ashes it carried with it.
>
> My uncle's scholarly acumen saw at once that it was important enough for a closer inspection, and he ordered a boat to be made ready, telling me I could come with him if I wished. I replied that I preferred to go on with my studies, and as it happened he had himself given me some writing to do.
>
> As he was leaving the house he was handed a message from Rectina, wife of Tascus whose house was at the foot of the mountain, so that escape was impossible except by boat. She was terrified by the danger threatening her and implored him to rescue her from her fate. He changed his plans, and what he had begun in a spirit of inquiry he completed as a hero. He gave orders for the warships to be launched and went on board himself with the intention of bringing help to many more people besides Rectina, for this lovely stretch of coast was thickly populated.

He hurried to the place which everyone else was hastily leaving, steering his course straight for the danger zone. He was entirely fearless, describing each new movement and phase of the portent to be noted down exactly as he observed them. Ashes were already falling, hotter and thicker as the ships drew near, followed by bits of pumice and blackened stones, charred and cracked by the flames: then suddenly they were in shallow water, and the shore was blocked by the debris from the mountain.

For a moment my uncle wondered whether to turn back, but when the helmsman advised this he refused, telling him that Fortune stood by the courageous and they must make for Pomponianus at Stabiae. He was cut off there by the breadth of the bay (for the shore gradually curves round a basin filled by the sea) so that he was not as yet in danger, though it was clear that this would come nearer as it spread. Pomponianus had therefore already put his belongings on board ship, intending to escape if the contrary wind fell. This wind was of course full in my uncle's favour, and he was able to bring his ship in. He embraced his terrified friend, cheered and encouraged him, and thinking he could calm his fears by showing his own composure, gave orders that he was to be carried to the bathroom. After his bath he lay down and dined; he was quite cheerful, or at any rate he pretended he was, which was no less courageous.

Meanwhile on Mount Vesuvius broad sheets of fire and leaping flames blazed at several points, their bright glare emphasized by the darkness of night. My uncle tried to allay the fears of his companions by repeatedly declaring that these were nothing but bonfires left by the peasants in their terror, or else empty houses on fire in the districts they had abandoned. Then he went to rest and certainly slept, for as he was a stout man his breathing was rather loud and heavy and could be heard by people coming and going outside his door. By this time the courtyard giving access to his room was full of ashes mixed with pumice stones, so that its level had risen, and if he had stayed in the room any longer he would never have got out. He was wakened, came out and joined Pomponianus and the rest of the household who had sat up all night.

They debated whether to stay indoors or take their chance in the open, for the buildings were now shaking with violent shocks, and seemed to be swaying to and fro as if they were torn from their foundations. Outside, on the other hand, there was the danger of falling pumice stones, even though these were light and porous; however, after comparing the risks they chose the latter. In my uncle's case one reason outweighed the other, but for the others it was a choice of fears. As a protection against falling objects they put pillows on their heads tied down with cloths.

Elsewhere there was daylight by this time, but they were still in darkness, blacker and denser than any ordinary night, which they relieved by lighting torches and various kinds of lamp. My uncle decided to go down to the shore and investigate on the spot the possibility of any escape by sea, but he found the waves still wild and dangerous. A sheet was spread on the ground for him to lie down, and he repeatedly asked for cold water to drink.

Then the flames and smell of sulphur which gave warning of the approaching fire drove the others to take flight and roused him to stand up. He stood leaning on two slaves and then suddenly collapsed, I imagine because the dense, fumes choked his breathing by blocking his windpipe which was constitutionally weak and narrow and often inflamed. When daylight returned on the 26th - two days after the last day he had been seen - his body was found intact and uninjured, still fully clothed and looking more like sleep than death.

In a later letter to Tacitus, Pliny went on to describe what followed to both him and his mother on the next day of the destruction of Pompeii.

Ashes were already falling, not as yet very thickly. I looked round: a dense black cloud was coming up behind us, spreading over the earth like a flood. 'Let us leave the road while we can still see,' I said, 'or we shall be knocked down and trampled underfoot in the dark by the crowd behind'. We had scarcely sat down to rest when darkness fell, not the dark of a moonless or cloudy night, but as if the lamp had been put out in a closed room.

You could hear the shrieks of women, the wailing of infants, and the shouting of men; some were calling their parents, others their children or their wives, trying to recognize them by their voices. People bewailed their own fate or that of their relatives, and there were some who prayed for death in their terror of dying. Many besought the aid of the gods, but still more imagined there were no gods left, and that the universe was plunged into eternal darkness for evermore.

There were people, too, who added to the real perils by inventing fictitious dangers: some reported that part of Misenum had collapsed or another part was on fire, and though their tales were false they found others to believe them. A gleam of light returned, but we took this to be a warning of the approaching flames rather than daylight. However, the flames remained some distance off; then darkness came on once more and ashes began to fall again, this time in heavy showers. We rose from time to time and shook them off, otherwise we should have been buried and crushed beneath their weight. I could boast that not a groan or cry of fear escaped me in these perils, but I admit that I derived some poor consolation in my mortal lot from the belief that the whole world was dying with me and I with it.

THE LESSONS OF JUDGMENT

Wherefore God also gave them up to uncleanness through the lusts of their own hearts, to dishonour their own bodies between themselves: Who changed the truth of God into a lie, and worshipped and served the creature more than the Creator. . . .
—Romans 1:25

In many respects, the people of Pompeii were just like modern Americans. They lived their private lives. They would go out to eat together. They had an economy. They held elections. They had little children. And they allowed tremendous debauchery. They had fallen into deep sin, and they were punished as a result.

When we live in or look at a nation fallen into deep sin, we need to realize that it deserves God's complete and immediate judgment. Apart from God's mercy, no nation would ever stand up to the test of God. But when we are wallowing in sin and perversion, we must expect judgment to fall.

America is a nation that has been enjoying a deposit of blessings which was created centuries ago. This deposit is almost completely gone. Today most people have forgotten the heritage of Americas founding and have cast aside the understanding of what it means to be a people set aside to the Lord. Because of this, we are standing in the path of judgment. We will eventually face the consequences of our own actions. Everything does not continue as it has in the past, and while we may not see pending destruction in the future, neither did Sodom and Gomorrah nor Pompeii anticipate their demise.

Isaiah 48:6-7 says:

> *I am the LORD, and there is none else. I form the light, and create darkness: I make peace, and create evil: I the LORD do all these things.*

History illustrates the awesome display of God's power in the carrying out of His eternal plans in perfect faithfulness to His words. It shows how God intervenes in the life of nations. When we study the Word of God, we can better understand what His revealed plan is for history. Part of this understanding involves recognizing that obedience to Christ means blessing; disobedience means judgment.

The more you understand the Scriptures, the only infallible history book in all time, the better man will understand the truth of this. The more man takes the truth of the Scriptures and applies it to history, the more man will know the reasons God sends judgment on a nation. When you seek to understand history in light of the basic principles, laws, truths, and covenantal structure of all of life, then you can get a firm grasp on what history truly means.

One of the words which we need to understand as Christians is the word "covenant." Unless we know the implications of what covenant means, we will not be able to truly understand the Bible. A covenant is a bond between two or more people. Man is in a covenantal bond with God. That bond is God's law as laid out in Scripture. When we obey his law, we are remaining true to the covenant. When we break His law, we are breaking covenant.

Everything that happened to God's people in the Old Testament happened because they lived in this covenantal context, and it happened because of some law, some threat, some promise, some act of faith, some act of obedience or disobedience. This was true during the days of the New Testament, and it is true of us today. That covenantal structure did not end with the Bible; it is still operative today. Everything good and bad happens because of the covenantal structure in which we live. Every person on earth is in this covenant and under the law of God, even though most people reject it.

We live in a world where our God controls everything that happens and has a purpose and plan for everything in life, whether it is good or bad. This is the only God. There is no other. God had a plan for the destruction of Pompeii, and that plan was to punish evil and to create an example for future generations of sinners. It was a display of God's awesome power forever carrying out his eternal plans in perfect faithfulness. Man didn't call Mount Vesuvius to erupt; God did. The destruction of Pompeii involved the judgment of God on some of the grossest perversion imaginable.

Apart from the mercy of God, we have no hope but to see the same end. And yet, we can be encouraged that God is in control, and our future will play out according to His will. It is not just a god who governs, but it is our God who governs. The gates of hell will never prevail against the church of the Lord Jesus Christ.

GROUP DISCUSSIONS AND QUESTIONS

1. What does "what goes around, comes around" imply about one's perspective on history?

2. What warnings had the people of Pompeii failed to heed? What are some similar biblical stories of God's warning for nations deserving judgment?

In the biblical examples do they repent?

3. Name four technological advances of the Pompeiians.

4. Are natural disasters accidents or a result of God's hand moving providentially through nature? Defend your position.

5. Since we are not seeing the actual remains of the dead people of Pompeii, what are we seeing?

6. What was it that killed Pliny the elder?

7. What is the message of Pompeii to Americans today? How do we need to learn from Pompeii?

LECTURES AND VIDEO SERIES

Audio: Pompeii: Suetonius and Tacitus, A Look at Julius Caesar and Octavian Augustus, Pompeii and the Destruction of Mount Vesuvius, Pompeii: Architecture and Home Design, Pompeii Part 2

Video: Day 3-Pompeii: Message on God's Sovereignty, Day 3-Pompeii: Walking Tour, Day 3-Wrap-Up

FURTHER STUDY AND RECOMMENDED READING

The Destruction of Pompeii by Pliny the Younger

The End of Empire: Attila The Hun & The Fall of Rome by Christopher Kelly

Complete Works by Tacitus

Christians and the Fall of Rome by Edward Gibbon

How Rome Fell by Adrian Goldsworthy

Rome, by Michael Grant

Foundations of Social Order by R. J. Rushdoony

PART II
GENEVA AND FRANCE

CHAPTER VI

FOUR CITIES THAT CHANGED THE WORLD OF CHRISTENDOM

INTRODUCTION: HOW CITIES BUILT CHRISTENDOM

The history of Christianity and Western Civilization can be traced by the providential direction of God through men and their ideas, through the battles that shaped the destinies of nations, and especially through the cultures that emerged either advancing or opposing the values of Christendom. But another way to trace God's providence over the last two millennia is by examining the great cities at the center of the most momentous and sometimes tumultuous events. We have already seen how one city—Rome— would change the world, continuing to influence men and nations long after its decline. In this part of our journey, we examine four cities, each of which had its season of prominence and far-reaching influence on the world.

Our journey will take us to Geneva, a city that once exemplified the Reformers call to the righteous rule of Christ over His people. From there we visit the city that once defined opulence and self worship—Versailles. Next, we travel to Paris, a city where the blood of martyrs, innocents, aristocrats and revolutionaries watered the streets. But first, we will begin in the small French city of Noyon where medieval kings rallied to build their empires.

Noyon: City of Kings

It is remarkable to consider that over a period of just under a thousand years, Noyon, now a sleepy little town in Northern France, served as a key location for three of the most important men of history—the man responsible for the emergence of the European states, the man responsible for the creation of France, and the man who has been described as the true founder of the United States of America.

Today Noyon is a quiet city an hour outside of Paris, but once it was the city of kings and leaders. At the heart of the city is the great Noyon Cathedral, on the site where the founder of modern Europe, Charlemagne, and the founder of France, Hugh Capet, were both crowned. It is also the site of the baptism of the great John Calvin, whose doctrine would transform the world.

The Crowning of Charlemagne

Known as the "Founding Father of Europe," Charlemagne was crowned King of the Franks in the Cathedral of Noyon in 768 A.D.

The son of Pepin the Short and the grandson of the famed Charles Martel, Charlemagne was a profoundly influential leader in his own right. Like his grandfather before him, he was a serious warrior. Charlemagne battled the Muslims with varied success, and following thirty years and eighteen battles with the Saxons, he subdued Saxony, forcing his defeated foes to convert to Christianity. He also conquered Bavaria, Carinthia, and the Lombard Kingdom and other parts of Italy, significantly expanding the

Frankish Empire to include much of Western and Central Europe.

In 799, after Pope Leo III had fallen out of favor with many in Rome, Charlemagne came to his defense and was rewarded the following year by being named Imperator Augustus—Emperor of the Romans—on December 25, 800 in St. Peter's Basilica in Rome. A zealous defender of Roman Catholicism, he took his role as Emperor seriously and sought to not only convert others to his faith but to spread Catholic culture in the realms he conquered. While he himself could not read or write proficiently, he had books such as Augustine's *City of God* read to him, and he actively promoted advances in scholarship, the arts, and architecture, with his cultural emphasis leading to what historians have called the Carolingian Renaissance.

An immoral man, Charlemagne encouraged his sons to engage in debauched behavior, and his worldview in many respects embodied all the wrong ideas that flowed from Rome: a sense of religious zeal, mixed with moral license—along with the trappings of icons and false worship and gestures of self-promotion that the Caesars championed. Charlemagne's efforts helped to define the Middle Ages and to forge a common European identity, yet this identity was one in need of much biblical reform.

A lament made upon his death by a monk of Bobbio illustrates both the regard his subjects had for him, as well as the conflicted worldview that his life represented:

> *From the lands where the sun rises to western shores, People are crying and wailing. . . . . the Franks, the Romans, all Christians, are stung with mourning and great worry . . . the young and old, glorious nobles, all lament the loss of their Caesar. . .*

The Capetian Dynasty

Hugh Capet, the father of the Capetian dynasty, was crowned King of the Franks in Noyon on July 3, 987. His coronation is widely regarded as the birth of modern France, due to the fact that, in his role as Count of Paris, he took the important step of centralizing power in Paris, from which he wielded influence over the rest of the country.

The Capetian dynasty is without rival in Europe, ranking as the largest and oldest European royal house. Branches of the House of Capet include the House of Burgundy, the House of Bourbon, and the House of Valois, among others.

Hugh Capet's descendants read like a *Who's Who* list of European royalty. Among his progeny are 3 Latin Emperors, 38 Kings of France, 9 Kings of Portugal, 11 Kings and Queens of Naples, 4 Kings of Sicily, 10 Kings and Queen of Spain, 12 Kings of Navarre, 3 Kings and Queen of Poland, 10 Kings and Queen of Spain, 4 Kings and Queen of Hungary—along with scores of princes and princesses, dukes and duchesses, and count and countesses.

During the French Revolution, the term "Capet" became a byword for capricious rulers, as King Louis XVI and Marie Antoinette—who came from different branches of the Capetian dynasty—were derisively dubbed "Louis and Antoinette Capet."

The Coming of Calvin

Of the three great men of Noyon, it would be John Calvin who had the most lasting impact on the development of Christianity and Western Civilization. Born in 1509, Calvin was probably the most important and influential man of the last millennium for the history of Christianity and Western Civilization. His careful defense of the sufficiency of Scriptures and the doctrines of grace, and his refutations of Romanism fueled the great Reformation. But it was the application of doctrines like the law of God, the priesthood of the believers, the importance of covenant, and more, which laid the philosophical foundations for the birth of the United States of America and the reformation of many other nations.

If we could look through a window into time's past, we might observe the year 1509, with Jeanne le Franc and Gerard Cauvin, the parents of John Calvin, watching over his baptism from the parish church of Sainte-Godeberte, not far from the very location where Charlemagne and Capet were once crowned. Just a few years later, we would see the young Calvin attending boys school in Noyon at the College des Capettes.

Today, the principle reminder of Calvin's origins on Noyon is the restoration of his birth house, located just yards from the Cathedral. This Museum of John Calvin was built in 1918 and founded by the History of French Protestantism Society. It provides a wealth of historical treasure about the Reformation in France, the friends and enemies of Calvin, the great persecution of Christians in Noyon that happened after the death of Calvin, and more.

LECTURES AND VIDEO SERIES

Audio: How Friendships Changed the World, The Significance of John Calvin, Overview of Noyon, Charlemagne

Video: Day 7-Calvin's Home, Day 7-Noyon

Geneva: City of God

While Geneva is known for many things today, including being a leading center for international banking and commerce, the home of Woodrow Wilson's failed League of Nations, as well as the birthplace of philosopher Jean-Jacques Rousseau, Geneva during the time of John Calvin became an incubator of a sound and developed biblical worldview and a light to the world unrivalled by any other city since the Apostles' time. Like the Zion discussed in the Scriptures, Geneva was a faithful "City of God" for a season that radically transformed the world, earning it the moniker, the "Protestant Rome."

The City that Feared God

Geneva has been a strategically important city from ancient times, located where the Rhone River empties into Lake Geneva. The city fell to Rome in 58 B.C., and Julius Caesar gives us the first recorded use of the name "Genua", a variation of the city's name. Burgundians, Franks, Merovingians, Carolingians, among other groups, controlled Geneva at different periods throughout its history.

By the early sixteenth century, the House of Savoy and the bishops of Rome were vying for control of the city. In 1513, Pope Leo X, in a clever move, appointed a new bishop in Geneva who also happened to be of the House of Savoy, thus uniting the ecclesiastical and civil powers.

Dissatisfied with this arrangement, liberty-minded citizens of Geneva eventually ejected the Duke of Savoy in 1532 and allied themselves with the Swiss Cantons of Berne and Frieburg, desiring to make Geneva an independent republic along the lines of these two cantons with which Geneva was in league.

Berne had declared itself for the Protestant Church, while Frieburg was staunchly Roman Catholic, which led to tensions in Geneva. The Protestant leader William Farel, a zealous preacher of the true Gospel, was sent from Berne to Geneva in 1532 in the midst of this controversy and was soon driven from the city due to his outspoken teaching against the false doctrines of Rome. But Farel returned when Geneva declared itself for the Protestant faith in late 1535.

In July of 1536, John Calvin, the twenty-seven-year-old scholar who had a few months before published his first edition of his *Institutes of the Christian Religion*, stopped in Geneva while on a journey, planning to stay only one night there. Farel, knowing of Calvin's impressive reputation, aggressively pressed his younger brother in the faith to stay and join the cause of reformation in Geneva with him. Calvin summarizes the scene as follows:

> *Farel, who burned with an extraordinary zeal to advance the Gospel, immediately strained every nerve to detain me. And after having learned that my heart was set upon devoting myself to private studies for which I wished to keep myself free from other pursuits, and finding that he gained nothing by entreaties, he proceeded to utter an imprecation that God would curse my retirement, and the tranquillity of the studies which I sought, if I should withdraw and refuse to give assistance, when the necessity was so urgent. By this imprecation I was so stricken with terror, that I desisted from the journey which I had undertaken; but sensible of my natural bashfulness and timidity, I would not bring myself under obligation to discharge any particular office.*

Calvin started out his service in Geneva as merely a "reader of Holy Scripture," but before long, he was elected as a pastor due to his obvious giftings. Farel and Calvin sought to implement significant changes with a new confession of faith and articles of worship which were approved by Geneva's city councils in early 1537.

Yet due to Farel's and Calvin's refusal to administer the Lord's Table to unruly citizens, as well as their refusal to denounce Courald, a fellow Protestant preacher in Geneva who the Council wanted removed from his pastoral office because of his fiery preaching, Farel, Calvin, and Courald were all three exiled from the city in April of 1538.

Upon learning of Calvin's expulsion from Geneva, fellow-reformer Martin Bucer invited him to come to Strasbourg and pastor a French-speaking congregation there that was in need of leadership. Calvin accepted Bucer's offer, and while pastoring in Strasbourg, he married Idelette de Burre, a widow in his church.

Meanwhile back in Geneva, the void of Calvin's and Farel's leadership began to be felt in this city that still desired to remain Protestant. The issue was heightened when Cardinal Sadoleto, a brilliant and respected Catholic scholar, wrote a compelling letter to Geneva, seeking to lure the city back to Rome. No one in Geneva was equipped to answer Sadoleto's arguments for the Catholic faith, so they petitioned Calvin to reply. Calvin's point-by-point refutation of Rome's star apologist completely obliterated his arguments and silenced him.

Calvin's feat in defense of the faith, along with other changes in Geneva's political scene, led officials to petition him to return in 1541. Reluctant at first, he eventually agreed under the condition that he would be allowed to implement comprehensive biblical reform. Summarizing the issue to Farel, Calvin wrote, "Immediately after I offered my services to the Council I declared that a church should be agreed on, such as prescribed for us in the word of God, and such was in the ancient church. . . ." Geneva's magistrates agreed, and Calvin returned.

Calvin moved swiftly in 1541 to make broad-sweeping reforms, drafting his Ecclesiastical Ordinances and creating a Consistory, a governing church body that adjudicated moral controversies and helped to counsel church members in matters of faith and practice. The following year, Calvin was appointed to a committee to revise the Geneva Edicts.

Yet wholesale change to the city's moral character did not happen overnight. Superstitious and immoral factions remained in Geneva, the most vocal being the Libertines, who consistently challenged Calvin's leadership. Calvin's perseverance, however, in faithfully preaching God's Word, ministering to the people, and holding the line on key issues eventually won out, so that by the middle 1550s, Geneva had been dramatically transformed into a city that feared God and modeled biblical Christianity in remarkable ways.

Prostitution was abolished. Laws were enacted to prohibit work on the Sabbath and to enforce just weights and measures. Reformed scholarly works proliferated, with thirty-four presses being active by 1563, prompting Catholic-controlled France to ban all books published in Geneva. The city became not only a hub of powerful ideas, but a haven for cultivating important godly friendships that changed the world, even as persecution raged in other regions. Fidelity to God's Word became a cherished priority in this "New Jerusalem" located on Switzerland's western border.

Upon coming to Geneva in 1555, English scholar and pastor William Whittingham described Geneva as "the mirror and model of true religion and piety." Scottish reformer John Knox was equally astonished at what he observed of Geneva's exemplary witness, noting the following to a friend in 1556: "This place . . . I neither fear nor am ashamed to say, is the most perfect School of Christ that ever was in earth since the days of the Apostles. In other places I confess Christ to be truly preached; but manners and religion to be so sincerely reformed, I have not yet seen in any other place besides."

Geneva's motto, "Post Tenebrus Lux"—After Darkness, Light—well-summarizes the massive change that God accomplished in turning the Geneva of Calvin's day from superstition and licentiousness into a model example for Christians the world over to learn from.

The Room that Launched a Thousand Churches

While Calvin preached and lectured at multiple locations in Geneva, no other meeting house more clearly signifies his global influence than the Auditoire of Calvin (also called Calvin's Oratory), a quaint 13th-century Gothic chapel located across from St. Pierre's Cathedral. It was here that Calvin regularly lectured to students who were part of his newly-formed Geneva Academy, many of whom went on to be missionaries and establish churches all throughout the known world.

The Auditoire was also the location that Calvin provided to Protestant refugees from around Europe to hold church services in their native English, Italian, Spanish, German, and Dutch. By 1557, Protestant refugees outnumbered the citizens of Geneva. Their flight to Geneva during this time was compelled in large measure by Bloody Mary's persecution of Protestants in England, Philip II's haranguing of Protestants in the Netherlands and Spain, and the De Medicis' and other radical Catholics' harassing of Protestants in France.

The Auditoire was the primary place these groups gathered for worship, including the English-speaking congregation that John Knox pastored while in Geneva. Leaders of Knox's church, including William Whittingham (who married Calvin's sister), Miles Coverdale, Christopher Goodman, and Anthony Gilby translated a new edition of the Scriptures from the original Hebrew and Greek into English—the Geneva Bible—which was published in 1560. This was this Bible that the Pilgrims and Puritans carried to America more than a half-century later—yet another example of how those who convened in Calvin's Auditoire effected massive global change for Christ.

To this day, Calvin's Auditoire represents the broad reach of his Reformed ideas, as the Church of Scotland (Presbyterian), the Dutch Reformed Community, and the Waldensian Church of Italy still hold regular worship services in the building, centuries after Calvin first lectured there.

This inscription on display in the Auditoire aptly summarizes its significance as a beacon of global influence: "In this nave John Calvin taught theology from 1562 to 1564 and his doctrine shone throughout the entire world."

The Reformers of Geneva

The Reformation Wall in Geneva provides yet another vivid illustration of Calvin's far-reaching and generational impact on world history, for not only does the monument feature key Protestant contemporaries of Calvin, but notable Calvinist leaders who championed his ideas and changed the world after his death.

The four most prominent statues on the wall, which are fifteen feet in height, feature the figures (left-right) of William Farel, John Calvin, Theodore Beza, and John Knox.

Farel, called the "Elijah of the Reformation," was short with a red beard that many thought well-represented his fiery character as a proclaimer of righteousness. Farel's strength was in his bold preaching. Philip Schaff writes:

> He turned every stump and stone into a pulpit, every house, street, and market-place into a church; provoked the wrath of monks, priests, and bigoted women; was abused, called 'heretic' and 'devil,' insulted, spit upon, and more than once threatened with death . . . . Wherever he went he stirred up all the forces of the people, and made them take sides for or against the new Gospel. No one could hear his thunder without trembling, or listen to his most fervent prayers without being almost carried up to heaven.

Born five years after Luther and Zwingli, Farel was twenty years Calvin's senior and was part of the first major wave of the Reformation, though he is best remembered as the man who secured Calvin's service in Geneva.

Calvin stands to the right of Farel on the Reformation Wall. The influence of Calvin is unsurpassed by any other figure from the Reformation. The impact of his tireless labors to systematize a comprehensive body of doctrine for God's people that presupposed Scripture as the final standard for faith and practice cannot be underestimated. Calvin's incomparable *Institutes of the Christian Religion*, along with his exegetical commentaries on the Scriptures, set a new bar for orthodox theological thought that transformed the world. Further, his emphasis on verse-by-verse exegetical preaching has inspired tens of thousands of preachers to faithfully exposit God's Word. Many more points could be added concerning Calvin's enduring legacy to Christendom.

While Calvin was recognized as the greatest theologian of his day, Theodore Beza, Calvin's close friend and eventual successor, was known in this period as the greatest orator of the Protestant cause. Born in France's old duchy of Burgundy, Beza, beginning in 1548, served with distinction as professor of Greek in Lausanne at a Protestant academy founded by another close friend of Calvin, Pierre Viret. Beza was a frequent delegate and spokesman on behalf of the Protestants at important meetings in Germany and France, and debated the Cardinal of Lorraine head-to-head on one notable occasion. Heavily involved in supporting the Huguenot cause in France, Beza joined Calvin in Geneva in 1558 as a fellow professor of theology and spent the final years of his life as Calvin's successor at the Geneva Academy.

John Knox, whose statue is to the right of Beza's, was a Scottish reformer who spent several years in Geneva with Calvin during Bloody Mary's reign. Upon coming to the true faith some years before, Knox served as the personal bodyguard to George Wishart in Scotland, wielding a double-edged broadsword in his mentor's defense while he preached. Following Wishart's martyrdom, Knox was captured and spent nineteen months of hard labor as a French galley slave, before being used by God in England and later, to great effect, in Scotland as a bold and uncompromising reformer. Knox's legacy of interposing magistrates (Mary, Queen of Scots, in his case) who disobey God's law was a key foundation stone in America's break from England several centuries later.

The smaller statues on the Reformation Wall include such men as Oliver Cromwell, whose challenge to Charles I's tyranny led to the monarch's eventual beheading, after which Cromwell became Lord Protector of England. A staunch Calvinist, Cromwell was used mightily by God as a defender of the faith.

Stephen Bocskay, known as the "Cromwell of Hungary" was another committed Calvinist who, after much wrangling, secured the Peace of Vienna in 1606 which guaranteed constitutional and religious rights for

Hungarians in Transylvania and Royal Hungary.

The Admiral Gaspard de Coligny, a contemporary of Calvin, led the Huguenot resistance movement in France in several wars. Well-respected by both friend and foe, he was greatly encouraged in his labors by Calvin's letters from Geneva, and was France's brightest hope as a leader until he was assassinated as part of the wicked St. Bartholomew's Massacre in 1572, which claimed the lived of tens of thousands of French Huguenots during a merciless killing spree.

The Admiral also had a global vision for colonization, and with Calvin's help, he planted a Huguenot colony in Brazil and another in Spanish Florida. While both settlements were short-lived, the Admiral's efforts to launch a beachhead for Protestantism in the New World presaged the profound impact that Calvin's theology would have on colonization in America with the coming of the Pilgrims and Puritans more than fifty years later.

Cotton Mather, the eminent New England Puritan of the 1600s, gave honor to Admiral Coligny on the opening page of his *Great Works of Christ in America* and referred to the Puritan's settlement as "another essay" that must be viewed in light of Coligny's efforts in the Americas the century prior. After honoring the Huguenots for their work, Mather noted that the Puritans' goal was to plant in America "Reformed Churches; nothing in doctrine, little in discipline, different from that of Geneva."

Thus, the leaders of the Massachusetts Bay and Plymouth Colonies such as John Winthop and William Bradford were Calvin's decided heirs and could have rightly been given statues alongside the Admiral Coligny and the other figures who are honored on Geneva's Reformation Wall. These American colonizers implemented the sound and sturdy biblical doctrines that Calvin and his associates hammered out in written works and modeled with their lives in Geneva.

Well it has been said, "No Calvin, no America." Harvard historian George Bancroft declared: "He that will not honor the memory, and respect the influence of Calvin, knows little of the origin of American liberty."

While many came and studied at the feet of Martin Luther, to whom

Calvin and his fellow reformers owed a real debt, Calvin's magnificent distillation of theology in his *Institutes* and *Commentaries*—which contain a more mature and consistent biblical worldview than Luther's—as well as his personal labors as a discipler and model of biblical principles in Geneva, left a profound impact on the world that exceeded that of his German counterpart.

John Adams, staunch patriot and second President of the United States, offered this summary and charge concerning Calvin's legacy:

> *After Martin Luther had introduced into Germany the liberty of thinking in matters of religion, and erected the standard of reformation, John Calvin, a native of Noyon, in Picardie, of a vast genius, singular eloquence, various erudition, and polished taste, embraced the cause of reformation. In the books which he published, and in the discourses which he held . . ., he proposed one hundred and twenty-eight articles in opposition to the creed of the Roman Catholic church. These opinions were soon embraced with ardor, and maintained with obstinacy, by a great number of persons of all conditions. The asylum and the centre of this new sect was Geneva, a city situated on the lake ancient, called Lemanus, on the frontiers of Savoy, which had shaken off the yoke of its bishop and the Duke of Savoy, and erected itself into a republic, under the title of a free city, for the sake of liberty of conscience. Let not Geneva be forgotten or despised. Religious liberty owes it much respect. . . .*

LECTURES AND VIDEO SERIES

Audio: How Friendships Changed the World, The Significance of John Calvin, Architecture: Transition from Rome to Geneva, The Reformers Monument, Geneva Evening Discussion, The Regulative Principle of Worship and How God Wants us to Worship Him

Video: Day 5-Calvin's Auditorium & St. Peter's Cathedral, Day 5-Reformers Museum, Day 5-Reformers Monument, Day 7-Calvin's Home, Day 7-Noyon

Versailles: City of Man

The city of Versailles, located ten miles west of Paris, is known chiefly for its famous chateau, the Palace of Versailles, which was built by Louis XIV, the Sun King, in an attempt to separate himself from the people of Paris, strengthen his power, and project his image as a god-like ruler of France.

Surrounding the Palace during Louis XIV's reign were the homes of thousands of courtiers and their retinues. In short, the city of Versailles was designed to serve the prerogatives of the king and to accomplish his every whim as an absolutist monarch. It represents the City of Man and those who desire to be as God.

The Worship of the Sun King

Louis the XIV, the King of France and Navarre remembered as the "Sun King", came to the throne in 1643 and reigned for seventy-years, longer than any other recorded European monarch. A staunch adherent to the Divine Right of Kings, he sought to arrogate greater power to himself and vaunt his self image through dazzling displays of extravagance through the obscenely opulent Palace of Versailles, a structure which had been a mere royal hunting lodge when he came to power.

His building campaigns at Versailles spanned several decades, with each one being more lavish than the last. Featuring over 700 rooms, the palace was self-consciously constructed and decorated to be an homage to his greatness, with numerous paintings and sculptures allegorizing his exploits with those of ancient generals such as Cyrus and Alexander the Great, and comparing him to pagan gods such as Jupiter and Mars.

The Palace of Versailles bespeaks one clear theme: Louis XIV is to be worshipped as a god.

The Return of Rome

Louis XIV's priorities at the Palace of Versailles also reflect a self-conscious return to Rome. On display are the wreath, the Roman fasces, and Roman-style architecture. The so-called "grandeur that was Rome" was ornately resurrected to take central focus as part of the grandeur of Versailles.

The War on True Religion

Versailles's religious themes represent a war on true Christianity and are nothing short of blasphemous. There are paintings with Gabriel and Hercules together, of Louis XIV interceding with the Virgin Mary.

In a sense, the building of Palace of Versailles marked the end of old order of Christendom and signaled the new order of Modernity that was about to sweep the world with the coming French Revolution, as Robespierre and his fellow Frenchmen revolted against the hypocritical faith that the Sun God sought to project at Versailles.

LECTURES AND VIDEO SERIES

Audio: Lessons from France: The Battle of Tours, Lessons from France, The Palace of Versailles Overview

Video: Versailles, French History

Paris: City of Blood

The Blood of the Martyrs: The Murder of the Huguenot Heroes

Today, when many think of French history they recall the story of the trial of Joan of Arc, the blood of the French Revolution, the conquests of Napoleon, and the tragedy and triumph of the Normandy Invasion. What is often forgotten is that France almost became a great beachhead in the West for the Reformed Faith. But all of that was thwarted in a single bloody day in the city of Paris during what came to be known as the St. Bartholemew's Day Massacre.

Here is the backdrop: Catherine de Medici's daughter, Margaret of France (Marguerite de Valois), had married Henry of Navarre (the future Henry IV of France), who himself was a Huguenot, on August 18, 1572. Huguenots from all parts of France had been invited to come for the wedding. It was hoped that this wedding would be an act of conciliation between the rival religious parties and end the warring between the Catholics and Protestants of France. Instead of a time for celebration, it would rapidly become a time of mourning for Protestants all over Europe.

Catherine had agreed to a plot hatched by the Guise family to assassinate Admiral Coligny, one of the leaders of the Huguenot party who had an influence over the king, Charles IX, her son. Providentially, the plot, attempted only a few days after the wedding and while the guests were still assembled, failed and only wounded the Admiral. Catherine was eager to complete the murder of Coligny and more, but anxious to hide her role in the scheme. She met in secret with her Italian advisers and Baron de Retz at the Palace of Tuileries to plan the massacre of all the unsuspecting Huguenots still celebrating in Paris.

On the night of August 23, Roman Catholics gathered at the Louvre in Paris and were given these instructions: to slaughter those Christians who maintained a belief in the sovereignty of God, the sufficiency of Scripture, the priesthood of the believer—those doctrines of the Reformed Faith which defined the cause of the Huguenots!

Just as the day broke on August 24, the massacre began. The Huguenots were pulled out of their beds and brutally murdered by the Catholic mob. Admiral Coligny was among the first to be killed. Henry de Guise, one of the instigators of the massacre, oversaw the murder of Admiral Coligny, and made sure that the "heretics" had finally been crushed.

The next day, the king issued a royal decree to stop the killing, but the massacre only grew. The blood lust of the Catholics spread all over France. The estimates of the number of Huguenots murdered has varied from 2,000, given by a Roman Catholic apologist, to 70,000, given by the Huguenot Duke de Sully, who himself barely escaped death. Historians today say that 3,000 were murdered in Paris alone.

Following the massacre, Pope Gregory XIII ordered a *Te Deum* to be sung as a "special thanksgiving" for the massacre. He also had a medal struck with this inscription "Ugonottorum Strages 1572" (Slaughter of the Huguenots) with an angel bearing a cross and sword beside the slaughtered Protestants. Paintings were commissioned and poems written to remember the "glorious execution." This is just a glimpse of the atrocities that were perpetrated against the French Protestants.

The Blood of Revolution: The Mania of Madame Guillotine

The French people had an amazing heritage of creativity, resourcefulness, and reformation, but as France moved into the age commonly called the "Renaissance," the nation would descend into a mist of humanism and darkness. From time to time, France would rise from this fog of humanistic principles and would return to its older foundations, but would then fall back into confusion.

During the American War for Independence, men like the Marquis de La Fayette would help to defend the cause of freedom which was being fought for in Thirteen Colonies. In fact, if France had not come to the aid of America in the way it did during the 1770s and 80s, the conflict would likely have had a very different outcome.

For decades leading up the French Revolution, the people of France had been living under an unjust and opulent dynasty of rulers who had used and abused their position of leadership. This sort of excess had caused many uprisings and clashes throughout French history, from the "White Hoods" of Paris in the 1400s to the revolution in La Vendee. While this helped the French to sympathize with the cause of the American patriots, their lack of Reformation grounding during the eighteenth century led them to swing to the opposite extreme of complete anarchy and mayhem.

As the American War for Independence came to an end in 1783, the clouds of revolution had begun to rumble in Paris, and by 1789, the National Assembly was formed, beginning the French Revolution. Sadly, unlike the American cause of liberty, the French Revolution was based around "man's inherent rights," not the God-appointed rights fought for by the Americans.

While the patriots in Massachusetts and Virginia were men who had inherited the legacy of their Separatist, Puritan, and Huguenot fathers, the French people had inherited the humanistic perspective held by the kings of France, the Voltaires, and the Rousseaus who had been some of the very ones to kick out the Calvinist Protestants and Huguenots in the sixteenth and seventeenth centuries. Because of this antithesis in origin, the French Revolution was attempting to attain a completely different notion of liberty. They were fighting for a man-centered "freedom," the type that revolved around *liberté*, *égalité*, and *fraternité* (liberty, equal rights, and brotherhood) that was completely divorced from God and His authority.

Because the French Revolution was birthed in humanism, it became a disgusting mass of bloodshed, lies, and atrocities to people of all classes. In the first three years of the revolution, the faulty and tyrannical monarchy that had ruled France for centuries collapsed into a mob of grotesque men intent only on their own gain.

The very air of France was transformed as the feudal, hierarchical, and religious statues were torn apart under the continual assault of the mob. The few remaining principles and thoughts that had been left over from the days of the Protestant Reformation in France were replaced by the new Enlightenment principles of citizenship. Because the Revolutionaries like Robespierre and Marat were trying to reject everything that was based around the old regime, both political and religious, they even went so far as to change the biblical calender and week. The new week was declared to be ten days long, a day ten hours, and an hour 144 conventional minutes. In short, they were trying to reject every aspect of their past, with special revulsion shown toward the created order of the universe that God ordained.

In September of 1792, the "Republic" was proclaimed, and radicals executed King Louis XVI the year after. The following two years marked the time in the French Revolution which forever after would be dubbed the "Reign of Terror," a title it deserves in every way. It is said that from 1793 to 1794, 40,000 people were slaughtered in the streets, and mainly at the feet of "Madame Guillotine." But as was the case in the Roman Republic itself, the very men who had helped to birth the "cause" would succumb to it, as Robespierre did on July 28, 1794, at the highpoint of French carnage. In 1795, the Directory assumed control of France and held power for four years when it was replaced by the Consulate, Napoleon Bonaparte in 1799.

Regrettably, the modern perspective on the French Revolution tends to view the atrocities committed during this uprising with rose-colored glasses. The same humanistic feelings that took hold of France before the Revolution began to take hold of England during the following century, as more and more people began to separate the understanding of God and his law from the proper response to tyranny. France's "enlightenment" would continue to twist and warp itself for the next hundred years. So many of the subsequent events in France can be traced directly back to the Revolution and its bankrupt theology—whether it was the Napoleonic Wars, the two moves to restore the monarchy, or even the two additional revolutions. France lost its foundation when it threw out moral principles and handed itself, bound, to the mob.

The Blood of Empire: The Failed Dream of Napoleon

He was born on an island and died on an island, but Napoleon Bonaparte became an adopted Frenchman who almost conquered the world. A Corsican by birth, he entered Paris for the first time in 1784 as a young, fifteen-year-old cadet who had earned an appointment at the prestigious Ecole Military Academy. A devoted student of war, Napoleon rose quickly in the ranks to second lieutenant, and after distinguishing himself in 1793 at the Siege of Toulon when he played a pivotal role in dislodging the British, he gained the rank of brigadier general as well as national acclaim in France.

On October 5, 1795, Napoleon was in Paris on assignment the day that the royalists attempted to overthrow the Directory. Gen. Paul Barnes, who was at the helm of the Directory's forces in Paris, ordered him to defend the Tuileries, and in pursuit of this end, he ruthlessly turned his artillery against the assembled mob, and in a "whiff of grapeshot" as Napoleon would later state, he scattered them. In reference to his bloody tactics, he coldly noted that "the rabble must be led by terror."

As a reward for this act of loyalty, he was given the prestigious post of commander of the Army of the Interior and was ordered to disarm Paris, which he obliged. Following distinguished campaigns in Italy and Austria, he turned his sites toward Egypt in 1798 in an effort to disrupt British trade routes as well as build his own personal fame. His prideful ambition is clearly evident during this campaign, as he mimicked Alexander the Great's example by including scientists and artists in his entourage. While his military conquest was curtailed when Lord Nelson's fleet obliterated his naval forces at the Battle of the Nile, his men discovered the Rosetta Stone and made other pioneering achievements in technology and exploration.

The following year, Napoleon returned to Paris and staged a *coup de tat*, unseating the Directory from power, after which he was named "first consul," which made him the virtual dictator of France. Napoleon's effectiveness as a leader earned him broad popularity among the people, and on December 2, 1804, in an incredible display of hubris, he took the crown from the hands of Pope Pius VII and crowned himself Emperor Napoleon I as part of a pompous coronation ceremony at Paris's Notre Dame Cathedral. To further commemorate his feats, he commissioned the world's largest triumphal arch to be erected in Paris, patterned directly after those in Rome that lauded the exploits of the Caesars. While the Arch de Triomphe would not be completed until after his death, it represents Napoleon's identification with Rome as well as his unbridled arrogance.

Amassing an enormous army, Napoleon then began efforts to conquer all of Europe. He had great success and gained control of Italy, Germany, Poland, and Sweden, among other European states, until Paris fell to the Allies on March 31, 1814, after which Napoleon abdicated as Emperor at Fontainebleau. Exiled to the island of Elba, he soon escaped and reinstated himself in Paris on March 21, 1815, beginning his Hundred Day's reign before he was decisively defeated on June 18 by the Duke of Wellington at the Battle of Waterloo. He finished his life in exile on the island of St. Helena, where he died on May 5, 1821.

One of the most successful military leaders in world history, Napoleon was not bashful to vaunt his victories, just as Alexander the Great and Julius Caesar had done centuries before. "Power is my mistress," he declared, and yet God humbled him in the end. "I should have conquered the world," Napoleon lamented. His lesson was the same as Nebuchadnezzar's: "the most High ruleth in the kingdom of men, and giveth it to whomsoever he will" (Daniel 4:17).

LECTURES AND VIDEO SERIES

Audio: Lessons from France

Video: Day 6-French History

GROUP DISCUSSIONS AND QUESTIONS

1. Who crowned Charlemagne Holy Roman Emperor, and what was the significance of him accepting this title? How did Charlemagne seek to implement his vision to advance the Catholic church, and what effect did this have?

2. The Bible says that "A good name is rather to be chosen than great riches, and loving favour rather than silver and gold" (Proverbs 22:1). Hugh Capet of the Franks had many descendants, but eventually his family name became a source of scorn and ridicule. How should this inform us in how we train the children in our family?

3. It took Calvin a good decade and a half before Geneva was transformed as a city. What does this teach regarding the need to persevere? Are you willing to stick to a hard task whenever results aren't immediately apparent?

4. What are some of the specific positive results that came from Calvin's labors in Geneva? Who were some of the man who came after Calvin who took his teachings and changed the world for Christ? How did Calvin's influence affect the founding of America specifically?

5. What is the legacy of Louis XIV and the Palace of Versailles? What was the reaction of the French people in the late eighteenth century to the opulence that Louis XIV created in Versailles?

6. What single act of villainy forever changed the Protestant cause in France, and what were the implications? What role did the Admiral de Coligny play in this episode?

7. Revisionist historians have gone to great efforts to draw comparisons between the French Revolution and the American War for Independence. It is certainly true that a handful of outspoken American Francophiles like Thomas Jefferson and the humanist Thomas Paine were initially favorable to the French revolutionary cause, but this was short-lived as reports reached the American people of the bloody Parisian tribunal and Madame Guillotine, revealing the true philosophy behind the movement. What were the religious, philosophical, and practical distinctions between the American War for Independence and the French Revolution?

8. In what ways have the philosophy and spirit of the French Revolution influenced movements in the twentieth century and beyond?

9. How should Christians interpret the life of Napoleon? Was he a hero or villain? Were his actions noble or despotic? Do his motivations appear to stem from personal ambition or a passion for the liberty of his countrymen? As a leader, is he more like George Washington, or Julius Caeser?

10. The Scripture says that Pharaoh actions may have been meant for evil, but God used them for good. During his conquests, Napoleon entered the land of the Pharaohs, an invasion that opened the door to the West of a treasure house of archaeological data. What were some of the most important artifact discoveries made in the wake of Napoleon's invasion of Egypt?

RECOMMENDED READING FOR FURTHER STUDY

Calvin and Geneva

Calvin's *Institutes of the Christian Religion* remains one of the most important works of theology in history and is must reading for the well-educated Christian student. Other helpful books on Calvin's life include:

Calvin: Man of the Millennium, by Philip Vollmer

The Genevan Reformation and the Founding of America, David Hall

Friends of Calvin, Michiel A. van den Berg

The Expository Genius of John Calvin, Steven Lawson

John Calvin for Young Readers

The Betrayal, by Douglas Bond

St. Bartholomew's Eve, by G.A. Henty

No Surrender, by G.A. Henty

Other Genevan Reformers / General Reformation

Illustrated Timeline of the Reformation

Reformation 500 Celebration (Audio Collection)

The Great Christian Revolution, by Otto Scott

History of the Reformation of the Sixteenth Century, by J. H. Merle D'Aubigne

History of the Reformation in Europe in the Time of Calvin, by J. H. Merle D'Aubigne

The Reformation: A Handbook, by T.M. Lindsay

Family Reformation, by Scott Brown

Reformation Heroes, by Diana Kleyn and Joel Beeke

Famous Women of the Reformed Church, James I. Good

Ladies of the Reformation, by J.H. Alexander

The Life of John Knox, by Thomas McCrie

William Farel and the Story of the Swiss Reform, by William Blackburn

The Protector [Oliver Cromwell], by J.H. Merle D'Aubigne

The Huguenot Heroes

The Huguenots or The French Reformed Church, by William Henry Foote

Gaspard de Coligny, by Walter Besan

Stories of the Huguenots in France and Italy for Young People

The Life of Jeanne d'Albret, by Martha Walker Freer

The Life of Marguerite of A'ngouleme, Queen of Navarre, by Martha Walker Freer

Vindiciae, Contra Tyrannos, by Stephanius Jurius Brutus

The French Revolution

Otto Scott's *Robespierre* may be one of the best histories written elucidating the criminal behavior and anti-Christian fervor of the French Revolutionary leadership. Dickens' *Tale of Two Cities* is the most powerful work of historical literature ever written on this time period. G.A. Henty's *In the Reign Of Terror* is an excellent introduction for youthful readers to the French Revolution. Yet another classic that takes readers of all ages.

Post-Revolutionary France

The Count of Monte Cristo remains one of the most important books of literature translated into the English language. Replete with Christian images and concepts, this book takes a look into the shattered life of a victim of the intrigues of the Napoleonic era, his escape from prison, revenge and restoration.

Victor Hugo's *Les Misérables*, though in no way a perfect book, paints an accurate and heart-wrenching picture of life during and after the bloody French Revolution. Though Hugo came to many conclusions which would not fit into a truly reformed worldview, he lived in an age when God's providential hand over all events in history was still understood. Victor Hugo also gives vivid and accurate depictions of the Battle of Waterloo from the French perspective and peppers the book with amazing details of the time and some very helpful retrospective commentary.

PART III
ENGLAND AND THE
RISE OF CHRISTENDOM

CHAPTER VII

THE ANCIENT WORLD MEETS CHRISTENDOM
A JOURNEY THROUGH THE BRITISH MUSEUM

THE ROLE OF MUSEUMS IN THE PRESERVATION OF THE KNOWLEDGE OF PROVIDENTIAL HISTORY

One of the primary purposes for museums is the preservation of the material cultures of civilization throughout time. People study and understand history better when they can see parts of history in front of them. They can learn about the follies and strengths from the past better when they can see it, touch it, and visualize it. Museums serve as a great means for this.

This said, museums are more than just a repository for storing historical facts and information. They also speak to the history of mankind and God's providential hand throughout time. Typically, museums try to cover the truth of providence behind philosophical words like "happenstance", "luck" or "Evolution". But ultimately, whether recognized or not, all history shows the glory and power of Christ over mankind throughout the ages.

Museums also have the privilege of holding pieces of antiquity which are not readily available for human interaction in any other place: artifacts like pre-Babylonian friezes and maps of the ancient battles recorded in stone carvings. These frozen "photographs" of history convey information that is not seen anywhere else in the world. Thus, museums preserve original knowledge in the sense that it is first-hand information which is not accessible in any other way.

But, artifacts like anything else, must be interpreted through the lens of a worldview. Interpretation is everything. Without a proper interpretation, facts cannot be rightly understood. Two different people can walk in to a museum and see the exact same thing and have two completely different perspectives on that object—one right, and the other wrong.

Sadly, many museums of the nineteenth century, such as the British Museum, were not only created to collect the antiquities of the past, but to self-consciously interpret them and present them in such a way that would lead us into the "new era of man" where we would not need the Bible and its history.

THE ORIGIN OF THE BRITISH MUSEUM

The British Museum is one of the greatest museums in the world and presents relics of history going all the way back into the pre-Babylonian and Egyptian times. It is truly a repository of some of the greatest artifacts of all time.

It was first established as the Montagu House in 1753, during the rise of Rationalism and Enlightenment thinking, when people were questioning the authenticity of the biblical account of Genesis. Rationalism swept through the universities and corrupted much of the clergy who were lured to ride the wave of intellectual advancement.

One of the foundational controversies of the time was chronology. The Rationalists knew if they could knock out the biblical chronologies, if they could assert that many of the stories found in the book of Genesis are fiction, then they could undermine the entire ethical system on which the Bible is based and destroy its applicability.

Moving into the nineteenth century and the early days of the British Museum of Natural History, the world was being even more fundamentally transformed by several influences: Unitarianism and Transcendentalism which swept through Europe and New England; German Higher Criticism, which came into the academies and said "that we will only believe those things which are in the Bible which we can prove through the external evidence, and which meets our autonomous reason"; and Darwinism.

But the heart of the debate was really over chronology, the one chronology supported the evolutionary hypothesis, and the other chronology supported the biblical hypothesis. The philosophical change in thinking was manifested by an attack on the length and origin of earth history, which was, in effect an attack on Scripture. This was where the modern fight for chronology began.

THE BATTLE FOR ARCHAEOLOGY, CHRONOLOGY, AND THE VINDICATION OF THE BIBLICAL RECORD

Both the archaeology and the nineteenth century museums played a pivotal role in the debate because the artifacts found were being used to justify evolution in the museums. By the twentieth century, it was more and more evident that the artifacts being discovered were actually supporting a biblical chronology and were even vindicating the stories of the Bible. The irony is that to this day we have never seen archeology repudiate the Scripture. To the contrary: Over and over again, we see archeology vindicating the Scripture instead.

By vindication, we don't mean "proof", because the Bible is self-authenticating; it doesn't need anything outside of itself to prove its validity. By vindication, we mean that the artifacts testify to the authority of God as spoken through the Scripture. The rocks themselves cry out as to the authority of the Scripture and as to the authority of what God has said.

Everyone has a worldview grid, a perspective on life which helps to interpret what they see. And it is our grid as Christians that gives us the conclusions we come to whenever we look at any historical detail or artifact.

It is this same principle, the principle of worldview analysis, which gives the evolutionist and humanist his perspective on life. When he comes to the table, he brings his perspectives derived from a grid which is not built around biblical principles.

As we begin to take a look at ancient artifacts, one of the first questions we must ask is how do we understand the time scale around which the earth and its history have developed? The Christian starts with the Word of God and a literal understanding of Biblical timeline and chronology.

The Bible gives us a number of epics in time, the first of which is the Pre-Flood World. All we can know today about the Pre-Flood World with any real accuracy is what is given to us in the Scripture. From the account in Genesis, we learn about the building of cities, the diversification of various dominion skills such as tent-making, the use of instruments such as the "harp and organ", brass and ironwork, and we learn that Cain had been a farmer and Abel a shepherd. But there is also much we do not know about the Pre-Flood World and its technology because of the Great Flood and God's judgment on the entire earth, which wiped out the memory of man.

The next Epic in time is the world before the tower of Babel. This time slot stretches from the days after the opening of the Ark and Noah's sacrifice to God to the time of the confusion at Babel. After the Flood we know of the division between the patriarchal line coming from Shem (Noah's son) and the descendants of Ham and Japheth who would be confused and divided at Babel. These were the days when the Earth was "divided", or explored and mapped as this term may well mean (Genesis 10:25). From our Christian and Creationist perspective, we would conclude that this Epic in time was very short, but that the Ice Age may have taken place during this time or directly post-Babel.

From the Tower of Babel onward we are introduced to the "Ancient World," our third Epic. The period of the Ancient World lasts from the post-Babel period all the way to the time of Rome and Christ, or "zero A.D.". The two-thousand-year time period from the time of Christ to the present is known as the "Modern World".

When we look at this chronology through a Biblical grid, we see the earth as approximately six thousand years old from Creation and the Pre-

Flood World to the present. This chronology is very different from the dates in most museums today because they are based off the presuppositions of an evolutionary and humanistic worldview.

What is so fascinating about archeology for the Christian is that we get to see the intersection between biblical chronology and the artifacts of ancient civilizations as they continue to match up and corroborate each other. We continually see that archeology upholds and vindicates the Scripture, and the British Museum provides many examples of this. Even through all the evolutionary dates and commentary on display there, we see the vindication of the Scriptures in the great artifacts of Biblical times.

GREAT ARTIFACTS OF THE BRITISH MUSEUM AND HOW THEY REINFORCE BIBLICAL TRUTH

As Christians, we know that understanding the past is the key to the present. Archaeology gives us a window into that past, disproving false speculations of previous eras, and showing us actual historical records and information from the ancients. We can look to many of the great artifacts of the British Museum as examples of this.

"The Black Obelisk" was discovered in 1845. This obelisk commemorates the triumphs of Shalmaneser III, an Assyrian king. One of the victories it mentions is the defeat of Ben-Hadad (King of Aram) and Hazael of Damascus, who are mentioned in 2 Kings 8 and 9. This obelisk also shows an image of Jehu, King of Israel, the man who dethroned King Ahab and Jezebel in 2 Kings 9.

In the Ancient World, significant events were often carved in stone. When we get to read the inscriptions on these stones, it is like reading from a history book. One such stone portrays tribute being sent by King Hezekiah, King of Judah, around 700 B.C., as recorded in 2 Kings 18. Another stone relief portrays "Sennacharib . . . king of the World," and the siege of Lachish which we read about in 2 Kings 18-19, 2 Chronicles 32 and Isaiah 36. Several monuments reference the Persian kings mentioned throughout the Bible like Cyrus, Darius, and Ahasuerus.

One particularly interesting stone is the Cylinder of Nabonidus which has helped clear up years of discourse on the subject of Daniel and Belshazzar of Persia, whom "experts" claimed never existed. But with the discovery of the cylinder, these experts found that Belshazzar had indeed been a real person and that he really was the son of King Nabonidus, and had been helping to rule at the time of Cyrus' takeover, as discussed in Daniel 5.

Each of these artifacts reflects the worldview and religious presuppositions of its time and nation as well. The mummies dating back almost to the time of Moses and the Israelites in Egypt reflect the Egyptian theory of the afterlife and their struggle to reach heaven and eternity by their own means. The Egyptians looked to the king as a god going to the afterlife, accompanied by servants, food, and other material possessions, ready to resume power in the next world.

Studying the stones in the British Museum, we clearly see the common origin that the pagan nations had in ancient Babylon mystery religions. Each of the pagan cultures have very similar accounts of the origin of the world, of a flood destroying the earth, and even of a Babel tower-like structure. The most famous of these is the flood tablet relating the Epic of Gilgamesh which is the Assyrian version of Noah and the Great Flood. Also on display is the cuneiform tablet with the Atrahasis Epic which gives the Babylonian version of creation and the flood. The records of all of these pagan societies point to events outlined in Scripture, though they pervert the Biblical story.

The list of amazing artifacts from the time of Abraham to the time of Christ housed at the British Museum goes on and on: a brick inscribed with the name of Nebuchadnezzar, King of Babylon, the Cyrus Cylinder, stone panels from the palace of Sennacherib, and the famous Rosetta Stone, which has been the key to breaking the codes of many different cultures. And yet, we are painfully aware that so much of the ancients has been lost. The destruction of the library of Alexandria, grave robbers, and natural disasters have all contributed to the loss of artifacts as well as our knowledge of the events of the past. Nevertheless, the British Museum is one amazing storehouse of historical and biblical information. The artifacts on display there are truly the rocks themselves speaking to the authority of the Scripture, just as Luke 19 says.

In some respects, archeology is the study of trash and rubbish, the study of left-over pots and shards after the robbers and natural disasters have swept through. But the more of this "rubbish" that is discovered, the more and more we will see the rocks crying out.

In the end, there are only two types of people in the world; those who worship the Creator and those who worship the creature. Those who worship the creature are willingly ignorant and will never truly be able to understand God's amazing providence in a place like the British Museum. On the other hand, those who worship the Creator will be able to see an amazing in-color picture of God's timeline throughout history when they see artifacts such as those preserved at the British Museum.

GROUP DISCUSSIONS AND QUESTIONS:

1. What is the Christian's key to understanding the present?

2. Why are Christians needed in the study of antiquities?

3. Whose soldier found the Rosetta Stone, and where did he find it? Explain the significance of the Rosetta Stone.

4. Who in the Scripture was sent to Assyria, one of the most ferocious and violent civilizations in history? From the images in the museum, can you speculate about why this man was hesitant about going to the enemy capital? Who destroyed the Assyrians? What is the message?

5. What is ubiquitous about the depiction of the gods of the ancient world?

6. The carving of Sennacherib's sacking of the city of Lachish shows what?

7. Describe siege warfare at this time.

8. The black obelisk of Shalmaneser III names King Jehu of the Bible. Read 2 Kings 17 and 18 and comment on the connection and the significance of the discovery of the obelisk.

9. Two artifacts, a limestone stela (a tall, carved, commemorative slab) to Baal and the Tanit Stela, both refer to a religious precinct, "the Tophet" which is described in the book of Jeremiah. Read Jeremiah 7 and 19 and comment on the connection and the significance of the discovery of

these artifacts.

10. What is significant about the brick of Nebuchadnezzar II?

LECTURES AND VIDEO SERIES

Audio: Archaeology and the Vindication of the Bible

Video: Day 8-The British Museum, Day 8-Wrap-Up

FURTHER STUDY AND RECOMMENDED READING:

Through the British Museum with the Bible, by Brian Edwards and Clive Anderson

Babylon Mystery Religion, Ancient and Modern, by Ralph Edward Woodrow

Newton's Revised History of Ancient Kingdoms, by Sir Isaac Newton

History of the World, by Bishop Ussher

CHAPTER VIII

THE ROMANIZATION
OF ENGLAND

THE ROMAN INVASION OF BRITON

The first Roman invasion of Briton came late in the summer of 55 BC, sent by Julius Caesar, the first Roman Emperor. It was intended as a reconnaissance-invasion expedition and only gained a foothold at what is now Kent. The second invasion took place the following year and was more successful. The Romans set up a puppet king, Mandubracius, over the Trinovantes and established Briton as a tributary province.

It is possible that the British Isles were explored as early as the fourth century by men like the Greek explorer Pytheas of Massilia. Pytheas made a voyage of exploration to northwestern Europe some time in 325 B.C. He is said to have visited a considerable part of Briton and is the first recorded person to speak of the midnight sun. But for all intents and purposes, the Romans were the first people to begin the modernization of Briton.

Caesar was extremely interested in this far off territory. He made reports on the different elements of British warfare which were foreign to the Roman people nine hundred miles away. He also made many geographical investigations of Briton. Whether these were made personally or based off of reports, Caesar's conclusions were generally accurate (in some areas more than others) and were extremely helpful for the formation of knowledge about Briton.

> The island is triangular in its form, and one of its sides is opposite to Gaul. One angle of this side, which is in Kent, whither almost all ships from Gaul are directed, [looks] to the east; the lower looks to the south. This side extends about 500 miles. Another side lies toward Spain and the west, on which part is Ireland, less, as is reckoned, than Britain, by one half: but the passage from it into Britain is of equal distance with that from Gaul. In the middle of this voyage, is an island, which is called Mona: many smaller islands besides are supposed to lie there, of which islands some have written that at the time of the winter solstice it is night there for thirty consecutive days. We, in our inquiries about that matter, ascertained nothing, except that, by accurate measurements with water, we perceived the nights to be shorter there than on the continent. The length of this side, as their account states, is 700 miles. The third side is toward the north, to which portion of the island no land is opposite; but an angle of that side looks principally toward Germany. This side is considered to be 800 miles in length. Thus the whole island is about 2,000 miles in circumference. —Caesar's Commentarii de Bello Gallico

THE GOSPEL AND THE SETTLEMENT OF BRITON BY THE ROMANS

Rome had first come to Briton to expand the Empire in its continuing attempt to control the whole world and bring it under the subjection and influence of Rome and its culture. But in the process, without being conscious of it, Rome spread Christianity through the slaves and families and even the soldiers who were being transported around the world. As "Roman towns" were established in different countries such as Briton and Caledonia, citizens moved into them and soldiers brought their families, often bringing the truth of Christ and the Gospel. Some of the slaves of Roman citizens in the first century were Christians. This was also true of some of the soldiers and even Centurions, as the Scripture shows in Matthew 8:5-13.

The Roman Emperor Constantine had an enormously significant impact on the spread of Christianity when he professed to convert to Christ and then synthesized pagan Roman practices with Christianity. Yet the Gospel was also enabled to come to Briton during the first few centuries before it reached many other places through the early Apostles and monks of Iona and other Irish missionaries.

The commerce that was established with various other parts of the world by Rome also created a steady stream of information and travel which only increased the spread of Christianity and the survival of the early Christians. God used the expanding Roman Empire to expand the boundaries of the Church, even in the first century.

One example of this is the story of Patrick of Ireland who was born sometime during the end of the fourth century, probably during the reign of Emperor Theodosius (347-395). Patrick himself said that his father was a "deacon of the church, and my grandfather . . . a priest." According to Patrick's writing his family lived in the village of Bannaventa Berniae, but "also had a country estate nearby." They were obviously well situated Romans who had settled and embraced Christianity. Philip Freeman in his book St. Patrick of Ireland says:

> *His family was part of the land-owning aristocracy of the island, an elite who controlled both the wealth of Britain's agricultural production and the power of local government, as well as the high offices of the emerging Christian Church.*

Patrick's grandfather, Potitus, was probably born early in the fourth century, during the reign of Constantine, the first "Christian emperor" of the Roman empire. It is likely that his family had at some point faced persecution, but they were now living in the relatively moderate days of the empire.

Patrick says that "I was led captured when I was just short of my sixteenth birthday, at a time when I had no real knowledge of God. I was led away as were so many thousands of others." He goes on to speak of how he had ignored the warnings of other Christians as to his soul. But it was while he was in Ireland that God began to turn Patrick's heart back to Christ.

He lived for six years in Ireland before making his escape home to his family. Having officially begun to work on the behalf of Christ, he returned to Ireland in the capacity of a bishop. It is thought that he worked in the north and west of the island, but at any rate, he was God's means to help transform Ireland into a semi-Christian country for a time.

Patrick is just one example of how the Roman invasion of Briton and implantation of Roman communities lead to the growth of the Gospel throughout Europe. Had the Romans not come and the Britons been left to their own devices, perhaps the history of the church would have been very different. But ultimately God's providence makes such speculations moot.

ROMAN TECHNOLOGY AND THE CREATION OF A NATION

As was the case in so many other Roman provinces, when Rome moved in, they brought their soldiers, their people, but they also brought their technology.

One of the great strengths of the Romans was their technological sophistication. When we look at all the great European cities of today, we see how the groundwork was laid by the technology of the Romans. Londinium was one of the great Roman towns in Briton. Today it is London, one of the biggest and most important cities in the world.

Here are a few well-known British cities that were originally Roman towns:

Bath - (Aquae Sulis)

Dover - (Portus Dubris)

Exeter - (Isca Dumnoniorum)

Gloucester - (Glevum)

London - (Londinium)

Manchester - (Mamucium)

Winchester - (Venta Belgarum)

York - (Eboracum)

The Roman town Aquae Sulis is now named Bath after the Roman baths which were built there. And York was where Constantine would be crowned emperor. Throughout Briton, we see the Romans' technological footprint.

The Romans also brought roads to Briton and created infrastructure for further conquest but, in England, as elsewhere, when Christianity came, it used the roads. It has been said that "whoever controls the roads controls the nation," and though Rome controlled the roads throughout the Empire, ultimately it was God who controlled them and who would use the roads for the greatest of ends—the spreading of truth. Due to Rome's road-building efforts, missionaries were able to travel easily and quickly in spreading the Gospel and this innovation in traveling technology created a realm of new possibilities. Centuries ahead of Christ's advent, God was laying His infrastructure through the Romans for the furtherance of the Gospel.

Many of the "advanced technologies" we use today, such as running water in our homes, toilets that flush, and baths, can be found in use two thousand years ago by the Romans. Modern man tends to think of himself as the most evolved or the highest up on the ladder of intelligence. But in reality we are simply standing on the shoulders of the men before us. In many ways, our forbears were way ahead of us technologically.

Yes, it's true that today we have computers and Internet, but who today could even make a basic running water system out of raw materials, let alone electric or computer technology? But the Romans did just that. They founded their empire off of the greatest technology of their day, creating viaducts and road ways, bridges and arches, baths and sewage systems everywhere they went! But ultimately not even the greatest technology can save man. Eventually the Romans were swallowed up in the tides of history just as every pagan nation will be which does not honor God. Yet their technology lives on.

CONSTANTINE: ROMAN EMPEROR AND THEOLOGICAL SYNCRETIST

Constantine is one of the emperors who continued the advancement of Rome into Briton, and who also helped the spread of Christianity.

Constantine was crowned emperor in York in 306 A.D. His crowning in York was really a statement to the world, done in order to testify that security could be found in the Roman Empire. Therefore he didn't have to be crowned emperor in Rome to show his capability and might. He didn't have to be in the capital city to be secure in his coronation. And neither did the people of the empire have to be in Italy; you could be in the farthest regions of the empire and be safe and secure in the arms of Rome. This was heresy, as Constantine was trying to tell the people of the world that security for a nation can be found in military or even political strength. Regrettably, this is a falsehood that we see our own political leaders even today seeking to propound.

We have a great deal to thank Constantine for as well as a great deal to regret about him, and we need to be careful to acknowledge both of these facts. Constantine professed salvation and confessed Christianity and was instrumental in stopping the ferocious persecution of the early Christian Church. But he also held onto aspects of his old faith: the sun god and other pagan beliefs, so he never fully understood the complete truth of the Gospel.

He also incorporated into Roman law some aspects of Christian law which, after his death, expanded into more and more laws particularly in reference to the family. But Constantine is really an enigma to us because of his syncretistic life. He thought he was a Christian and was willing to do whatever he thought Christ would have him to do. He stopped the persecution of the church, but he synthesized it as well and brought it into blended Christianity with various forms of paganism. So, to be honest students of history, we have to acknowledge both the good and the bad throughout Constantine's life.

GROUP DISCUSSIONS AND QUESTIONS

1. What was Rome's interest in Briton?

2. Finish the sentence: Whoever controls the roads, controls the _____.
   Explain what this means.

3. Where is the two-thousand-year legacy of the Roman Empire physically manifested throughout Europe, even into England?

4. How should we apply this to our lives in America today? Are there jurisdictional issues we should be considering?

5. Name three technologies left over from the time of Rome.

6. Summarize the story of Patrick. How does his story testify to God's providence?

7. Where was Constantine crowned Holy Roman Emperor? What statement was he making by choosing this location?

8. What is Constantine's greatest legacy?

LECTURES AND VIDEO SERIES

Audio: York and the Statue of Constantine, Medieval Walls

Video: Day 10-Welcome to York, Day 10-York Minster, Day 10-The Walls of York, Day 10-Wrap-Up

FURTHER STUDY AND RECOMMENDED READING

Beric the Briton, by G. A. Henty

Beric the Briton, by G.A. Henty (Audio MP3-CD)

Hostage Lands, by Douglas Bond

Life in a Medieval Village, by Frances and Joseph Gies

Life in a Medieval Castle, by Frances and Joseph Gies

The World We Have Lost: England Before the Industrial Age, by Peter Laslett

The History of England, by Thomas Babington Macaulay

Religion and the Decline of Magic, by Keith Thomas

CHAPTER IX

KING ALFRED, THE RISE OF CHRISTENDOM, AND THE MEDIEVAL FORTRESS CITY OF YORK

ALFRED THE GREAT

Over the history of the development of Christendom, few men have had such a lasting impact as a young prince-turned king by the name of Alfred. It is both interesting and important to note that King Alfred is the only king in the history of England that was given the title "Great", and he is the only king who has truly deserved that title. In the ninth century, Alfred would organize his men, drive the Vikings from strategic centers and locations throughout England, and most importantly establish the law rule of Holy Scripture as the foundation of the newly-established common law.

Today we remember Alfred for many things: his illustrious war song in which he cries out, "Jesu, defend us!" invoking the name of Jesus Christ as his soldiers would go into battle against the pagans. We remember him for the profound impact he had on the development of the castle cities of Europe which were made possible as a result of his subjugation of the land

and unification under the banner of Christianity.

It is hard to overestimate Alfred's importance for England, Europe, and even America. He not only drove the Danes out, but his support of Gospel missions resulted in the conversion of his enemies in many different places. Alfred established the tradition of a Christian monarchy and understood the basic principles Christ had laid out in the Scripture and was His tool in guiding the course of history.

He created a military defense program for southern England which was both innovative and very effective against England's enemies. This defense program was used against the Vikings, and after conquering them, he attempted to lead their leaders to Christ. One example was a Norse leader, Guthrum, who reportedly converted to Christ and was then baptized by Alfred. Whether Guthrum was truly converted or not it, is important to note that this man kept his oaths to Alfred and never attacked the English for the rest of his life.

Alfred advanced education throughout England. He also advanced literature, but particularly Christ, Christianity, and the Gospel. He would search all over England for great preachers and Christian scholars and bring them back to England to teach the priests and bishops and the people the true Christian faith. He even personally translated a couple of books by Augustine into English.

Once when Alfred was translating one of Augustine's books, a very small book, he took a great deal of time in studying the subject. By the time he finished translating it into English, he had lengthened Augustine's work by three or four times the original length. He had become so interested in his studies that he had not differentiated between his inserts and Augustine's original work! This is a story that really speaks to Alfred and his love for the truth of God's Word.

But Alfred's greatest influence was and always will be the codification of Old Testament law as the foundation for Christian common law. Drawing extensively from books of the Bible like Exodus and Deuteronomy, Alfred required that the principles of restitution and the fundamentals of biblical tort law become the law of the land.

This insured a foundation from which freedom and equity for all men could proceed. Alfred's codification became the basis for a thousand years of common law. Today we study the common law, and it plays a vital role in our understanding and whole approach to jurisdiction and law. So much of common law still coincides with Biblical law and this is because the common law had its roots in King Alfred the Great's theonomic law code. But for Alfred, we might never have seen the nobles take a reluctant Prince John and require him to sign the Magna Charta on the fields of Runnymede. Alfred therefore has rightly earned the title, King Alfred the Great.

KING ALFRED'S WAR SONG

When the enemy comes in a'roarin' like a flood,
Coveting the kingdom and hungering for blood,
The Lord will raise a standard up and lead His people on,
The Lord of Hosts will go before defeating every foe; Defeating every foe.

> *For the Lord is our defense, Jesus defend us,*
> *For the Lord is our defense, Jesu defend.*

Some men trust in chariots, some trust in the horse,
But we will depend upon the Name of Christ our Lord,
The Lord has made my hands to war and my fingers to fight.
The Lord lays low our enemies, but He raises us upright;
He raises us upright.

> *For the Lord is our defense, Jesus defend us,*
> *For the Lord is our defense, Jesu defend.*

A thousand fall on my left hand, ten thousand to the right,
But He will defend us from the arrow in the night.
Protect us from the terrors of the teeth of the devourer,
Imbue us with Your Spirit, Lord, encompass us with power;
Encompass us with power.

> *For the Lord is our defense, Jesus defend us,*
> *For the Lord is our defense, Jesu defend.*

YORK: SEAT OF AUTHORITY, COMMERCE, AND MILITARY STRENGTH

Of all the remaining medieval cities in Europe, none has as great a right to bear the title "The Medieval City" as does the fortress stronghold of York. York was first built by the Romans during the first century AD, was occupied by Vikings, Normans, and Goths, and would eventually emerge as the industrial, military, and strategic centerpiece of all of England.

Much of York looks the way it did close to a millennium ago. The original Roman walls are still there. The narrow stony streets highlighted by specific craftsmen, artisans, and vendors, are well represented in what is today still called "the Shambles". When we think of a medieval city and what it may have looked like, we think of York. Whether we realize it or not, that romantic-yet-warlike city that first comes to mind is the city of York. And this is because it fits all the classic elements for the ultimate "castle town": the great cathedral, the military fortress, the streets hustling and bustling, dirty, narrow, just as they might have been many hundreds of years ago. In fact, many filmmakers and artists have designed their art after the city of York.

York truly is a place of wonderment, not just because of its quaintness, but also because of its history. It is in York that one meets Constantine, on the very location where he was crowned emperor of the Roman Empire in the fourth century A.D. In York, one is also introduced to the Viking hordes, which once conquered and occupied the streets. In York, one sees the early Roman settlement and the ongoing influence of Rome through the vision of military fortification which continued and was maintained for close to two millennia.

York truly does exemplify the tale of England: once ruled by barbarians, then taken by the Romans, turned into an important thoroughfare for British commerce, then transformed into a medieval city that held the border between England and Scotland. York really does have it all.

YORK AND THE GUILD SYSTEM: A LESSON IN FREE-MARKET ECONOMY

York was also a great seat of commerce during the "old days" in England. For a thousand years or more, it was the home to the guild system which protected trades and crafts. By "guild system" we mean a trade association, an organization of craftsmen for a particular trade. These were private associations created to support the members in difficult as well as prosperous times. As a member of a guild, one had to work his way up through the system, proving his ability along the way.

The guilds were privatized and self-governing, a real example of how free-market economics can safe guard a society. Under this system of commerce, professional standards were set by the tradesmen themselves, by the master craftsman. Protocols were created to facilitate rising from level to level, ultimately achieving the position of master.

It was not a perfect system. The guilds got in trouble when they began setting prices and saying that tradesmen couldn't charge more than a certain amount. That brought about some controversy and difficulty. But the professional standards set and the system of self government were two of the great advantages. This is something that no socialistic government will ever be able to accomplish.

Once upon a time in America, we had the equivalent of a guild system to train our attorneys in the legal profession. At the time of the founding fathers, Patrick Henry sat before George Wythe to be examined to determine his eligibility to practice law. But there was no national bar, no national requirement. He was examined by his superiors within his trade to determine his competence. One of the benefits of this method is that it is not controlled by the state: it is a self-governing system to maintain excellence which brings longevity and stability and accountability to the craft and the culture.

In America today, we are moving toward socialization and state regulation and control. When you have state regulation and control, whatever the philosophical guidelines are that the state believes are a priority are then imposed on an entire industry. It is hard for us to imagine a system where the state did not regulate. We wonder who would be in charge. How would it work? Would there be mayhem and chaos?

The answer is that, rather than resulting in chaos, we would move to self-regulation, self-governance, more options for the consumer. In the free market economy, these solutions naturally emerge and work very well.

YORK: THE FORTRESS CITY

There are few finer examples of a walled fortress city than York. York is defined first and foremost by the walls which circumnavigate the city itself, walls whose history goes back more than a millennium. All around the city are these massive stone walls which have stood for century after century. The walls also have four main gatehouses or entrance ways to the city. These are the "Bootham Bar," the "Monk Bar," the "Micklegate Bar," and the "Walmgate bar." Each of these are beautiful examples of medieval-style architecture.

First constructed by the Romans in the first century, the walls of York would expand and continue their growth for the next thousand years. In A.D. 866, York was overcome by the Vikings who buried the existing walls and put up palisades. In the thirteenth century, the stone wall, which we see today, was erected. Eventually, the walls began to fall into disrepair, but to this day the remnant we see is magnificent and impressive. York truly has the feel of an ancient village film set.

Throughout the history of England, the walls of York have played a central role in the great battles and cultural changes that have seen this city go from the hands of Romans, to the Saxons, to the Vikings, to the Danes and Normans. York endured sieges, saw old cultures destroyed and new cultures rise up, and developed a thriving culture of its own. In a very real sense, the walls of York are an iconic representation of the changing nature of English society during the rise and fall and rise again of Christianity and Western Civilization.

The walls of York are also a reminder of many of the principles which we find within the Scripture. The Bible is replete with examples of and lessons based on walled cities. We read of the importance of tearing down the pagan high places, and this often included their walled cities as well as their temples. We think of the importance of rebuilding from the foundations the great walls of the cities of God, as in the case of Nehemiah. But in the end, we know that the armies of men, their fortresses and their walls—none of these things can ultimately defend against the greatest invader of all, sin within a nation. The Bible shows through and through that its not might, its not the power of man, but it is God alone that gives us the victory, just as Zechariah 4:6 says.

GROUP DISCUSSIONS AND QUESTIONS

1. What was important about the Battle of Hastings? Who were Harold and William?

2. What are the qualities of the English language which have helped it become predominant?

3. Norsemen conquered in accordance with their worldview. Explain this.

4. Name four people groups who conquered and inhabited York.

5. King Alfred the Great rallied England at the time of the Norse invasions and brought the tribes of the Anglo Saxons together, creating a kingdom with a king. What did he use as the basis for the law of the land? How long did this legal tradition continue? Why is this notable?

6. What is Alfred's War Song? What is unique about it?

7. The analogy of a walled city is used repeatedly in the Scripture. Proverbs 25:28 says: "He that hath no rule over his own spirit is like a city that is broken down, and without walls." Isaiah 58:12 talks about repairing the walls and foundations, and Isaiah 60:10 warns about strangers building the walls. The whole theme of Nehemiah is repairing the walls of the city. With these passages in mind, reflect on the city walls of York, which for at least a thousand years have surrounded the city. Consider all the nation groups which have used those walls, repaired them, defended them, been protected behind them. What do you learn?

8. Describe siege warfare at this time and compare it to the siege warfare of the Assyrians.

9. Describe the guild system and its benefits. Relate it to the free market and self government.

LECTURES AND VIDEO SERIES

Audio: The Guild System, York and the Statue of Constantine, The Norman Invasion, The Vikings, Medieval Walls

Video: Day 10-Welcome to York, Day 10-York Minster, Day 10-The Walls of York, Day 10-Wrap-Up

FURTHER STUDY AND RECOMMENDED READING

The Dragon and The Raven, by G.A. Henty

The Dragon and the Raven, by G.A. Henty (Audio MP3 & CD)

Wulf The Saxon, by G.A. Henty

Wulf The Saxon, by G.A. Henty (Audio MP3 & CD)

Life in a Medieval Village, by Frances and Joseph Gies

Life in a Medieval Castle, by Frances and Joseph Gies

The World We Have Lost: England Before the Industrial Age, by Peter Laslett

The History of England, by Thomas Babington Macaulay

The White Horse King, by Benjamin Merkle

Sabers, Spears, and Catapults (Audio CD)

CHAPTER X

THE REFORMERS, THE PILGRIMS AND THE FOUNDING OF AMERICA

THE RISE OF REFORMATION IN ENGLAND

The beginning of the Reformation is often traced back to October 31, 1517, when Martin Luther nailed his Ninety-Five Theses to the door of the Wittenberg Church in Germany. And while this was the beginning of the Reformation in the sixteenth and seventeenth century, the origins of the Reformation go back even further than Martin Luther.

Beginning in the twelfth century, a spiritual fire was sparked. It started near the Alps of Switzerland with a group of individuals named the Waldenses. This small, rag-tag group who believed in the sufficiency of Scripture and held that the Bible, not the bishop of Rome, had the final say in the understanding of doctrine, of orthodoxy and practice would fuel a fire that would then be embraced by others. Martin Luther would later invoke the name of the Waldenses as his true spiritual fathers. What took place in Switzerland and what was taking place in Germany would soon spread to England itself.

God always uses unusual means to advance the church of Jesus Christ. The message of history is always clear: that the gates of hell will never prevail against the church of Jesus Christ. This understanding was the fuel that kept the Reformation alive in the castles and the universities and the churches throughout Europe in the sixteenth and seventeenth centuries.

As with most great works of God, the English Reformation began with the dissemination and translation of the Word of God. For this, we can give thanks to a man by the name of Johannes Gutenberg whose invention of the printing press allowed for the dissemination of the Word. In the nineteenth century, Victor Hugo, himself a Catholic, commented:

> *Before the invention of printing, reform would have been merely a schism; printing converted it into a revolution. Take away the press; heresy is enervated. Whether it be Providence or Fate, Gutenberg is the precursor of Luther. —Victor Hugo*

But it wasn't enough for the Word to be printed. It had to be translated. In 1382, John Wycliffe translated the Bible from the Latin Vulgate into the common "lower English" which would completely change the course of events for the fourteenth century.

Wycliffe, born sometime in 1324 in Yorkshire, was one of the early English reformers to find fault with the extra-biblical teachings and heretical doctrine of the Roman church in the 14th century. In 1381, he wrote his very short doctrine of the Lord's Supper, which was in opposition to the Catholic view of the Eucharist. The chancellor of the University of Oxford promptly had Wycliffe's positions declared heretical and dismissed him from the University for his theses and his criticism of the Roman church.

As more and more men began to understand the truth of Wycliffe's teaching, they began to be called "the Lollards," which meant mumblers or murmurers since they were mumbling against the church. By the fifteenth century, the term had came to be synonymous with heretic. The Lollards preached that the Bible alone was enough to understand and know God, and that the Catholic Church was teaching heresy. Previous to Wycliffe, most people had only had access to biblical teaching through the Catholic priests or in the Latin translations. But Wycliffe's translation had made the Bible accessible to the common man. So the translation of the Scriptures was the fuel for the Reformation. Wycliffe was truly deserving of his title, "The Morning Star of the Reformation."

Truth is always purified and tried with fire. Throughout the Reformation, there was great persecution for those resisting the strangle hold of Catholicism. William Tyndale was another extremely important Reformation Bible publisher and was the first man to translate the Bible into English directly out of the original Hebrew and Greek. In 1536, Tyndale was betrayed, tried on a charge of heresy, condemned to death and "was tied to the stake, strangled by the hangman, and afterwards consumed with fire."

Tyndale's last words as recorded by John Foxe were "Lord! Open the king of England's eyes." It is amazing to note that within four years, his prayer had been answered, and at King Henry's behest, four English translations of the Bible were published in England, each version based off of Tyndale's own translation!

Men like John Wycliffe and William Tyndale sacrificed their lives fighting for translations of the Bible for the use of the common man. By making the Bible accessible, every single person, and not just the priests and prelates, could study the Word of God on their own, and biblical scholarship began to rise.

What had begun as a reformation-fire in the mountains of Switzerland, would be birthed in the life of men like John Hus in Bohemia and Ulrich Zwingli in Zurich, and would be embraced and dramatically advanced by a man named Calvin from Noyon, France, and eventually would come all the way to the court of Henry VIII of England. God used the hardness of man's heart to free the people of Israel. So too, God used the profligacy and argumentative nature of Henry VIII, who desired to be free from his marriage to Catherine of Aragon, a Roman Catholic, to force the question of the supremacy of the Catholic Church in England.

Henry, an immoral and prideful man, had been an instrument of persecution and division, but was rapidly becoming an unwitting tool by which God fanned the flames of reformation. Thus began the great and historic split between Rome and the English church, as Henry declared himself to be the head of the church in England. This was the first step in the history of a nation which would be beset by persecution and martyrs, victories and losses, on the reformation road.

In October 1555, under the reign of Henry VIII's daughter, Queen Mary Tudor, reformers Hugh Latimer and Nicholas Ridley were burned for accepting the Scripture as the ultimate authority and rejecting the Roman church. When they were brought to the stake, Ridley embraced Latimer and said, "Be of good heart, brother, for God will either assuage the fury of the flame, or else strengthen us to abide it." They then knelt together in prayer.

In describing this incident, John Foxe wrote

> A lighted fagot was now laid at Dr. Ridley's feet, which caused Mr. Latimer to say: "Be of good cheer, Ridley; and play the man. We shall this day, by God's grace, light up such a candle in England, as I trust, will never be put out."
>
> When Dr. Ridley saw the fire flaming up towards him, he cried with a wonderful loud voice, "Lord, Lord, receive my spirit." Master Latimer, crying as vehemently on the other side, "O Father of heaven, receive my soul!" received the flame as it were embracing of it. After that he had stroked his face with his hands, and as it were, bathed them a little in the fire, he soon died (as it appeareth) with very little pain or none.

Thousands were martyred during the Reformation, including three hundred during Queen Mary's reign alone. But Bloody Mary's persecutions only continued to increase the number of believers—God does use the blood of the martyrs as the seed of the church.

The 16th century brought to England many Bible translations, the proliferation of the preaching of the Word of God, and most importantly, the rise of Puritanism. Puritanism, with its focus and emphasis on the purity of the Word of God, the sufficiency of Scripture, and the doctrines of Grace, would give the church some of the greatest men in its two-thousand-year history: men who, like Cranmer, disseminated sermons among the priests which were then embraced by common men like John Bunyan, the author of *Pilgrim's Progress*. And ultimately was manifest in the life of the truly great Oliver Cromwell, under whose interregnum protectorate, England saw a golden season of doctrinal orthodoxy and the blessing of God.

HOW CONSPIRACIES OF FRIENDSHIP CHANGE THE WORLD

The more we study history, the more we see that history has never been made by majorities, but by dedicated minorities. In few places is this as clear as in the story of the Reformation. In Geneva and France we see how relationships like Viret and Calvin, with their extensive correspondence and mutual high esteem, were instrumental in establishing the schools of discipleship like the school of Calvin at the Auditoire de Calvin in Geneva where men like Knox were discipled and hundreds of churches were birthed. This was also true in England as reformation leaders supped with one other, wrote to each other, intermarried into each others families, and encouraged one another during times of ferocious and fierce persecution.

One particularly glorious vision of this "conspiracy of friendship" is found at Grimsthorpe Castle in the story of the great Lady Catherine Willoughby. Some of the greatest reformers of the day would be cared for at Lady Willoughby's home. Men like John Day, publisher of Foxe's Book of Martyrs, whom she subsidized, and Martin Bucer were regular guests at Grimsthorpe Castle, and Hugh Latimer spent a winter at the castle preaching.

They all came to Grimsthorpe Castle. They taught Lady Willoughby's children. They preached in the chapels. And they, in turn, were comforted and encouraged. Lady Willoughby was arguably the most vocal and active of the Protestant English noble women during the sixteenth century. Because of this, she and her second husband Richard Bertie were forced to flee England as refugees during the reign of Bloody Mary. Their story would be incorporated into a later edition of Foxe's *Book of Martyrs*.

During their time in exile, Lady Willoughby gave birth to a son, Peregrine, "pilgrim", Bertie. Peregrine would later become known as the "Brave Lord Willoughby" and became a ferocious defender of the Reformed faith. He would fight alongside the French Huguenots with great success, and he became one of England's most feared swordsmen. With only 1,500 men, he defeated 40,000 Spaniards at Flanders. In the ballad Lord Willoughby, the poet captured Willoughby's perspective on Providence as he sought to instill hope and inspire courage in his fellow countrymen:

Then courage noble Englishmen,
And never be dismayed;
If that we be but one to ten,
We will not be afraid

To fight with foreign enemies,
And set our country free;
And thus I end this bloody bout
Of brave Lord Willoughby.

Perhaps one of the most significant points about Lord Willoughby's life for those of us Americans is that he would go on to mentor a young man named John Smith. Yes, the same John Smith who would help to map and found the new country of America. As a boy, Smith spent time at Grimsthorpe Castle, sharing adventures with Willoughby's sons. John Smith not only gained a love for adventure and action from Lord Willoughby, he also learned to have an "unflinching trust in God's providential faithfulness" in all things. This is, in part, what enabled him to become the great explorer who helped to birth a new country.

Catherine Willoughby and her home, Grimsthorpe Castle, represent one element of many great "conspiracies of friendships" that would change the world and fuel the fires of the reformation. In the end, were it not for Catherine Willoughby, who raised up a son, Peregrine Willoughby, who mentored John Smith, America would have been a very different nation.

THE REFORMATION INFLUENCE OF BOSTON AND SCROOBY: THE PILGRIMS AND THE PURITANS

America was founded by a group of people who came from essentially two places: Boston and Scrooby, England. These were the two locations that birthed what one person described: "the single greatest spiritual revival in history." It is one of history's great ironies that some of the most obscure towns and villages have produced some of the greatest men with the most far-reaching impact. This is the story of Boston, England.

When most people think of Boston, they think of Massachusetts, where Puritan forebears like Cotton Mather, and later, men like John Adams would help to build and change the course of a new nation which would ultimately be called these United States of America. But the American city finds its origin, both spiritually and historically, in the first Boston.

It was in Boston, England that many of the greatest and most significant Puritan leaders were born: men like Edward Winslow and John Winthrop, the man who gave us the immortal expression "City on a Hill" and who became one of the first governors of Massachusetts; men who were part of the "spiritual brotherhood" of reformers. Boston was the city of John Cotton, John Foxe, the author of Foxe's *Book of Martyrs* and Anne Bradstreet, the Reformation poetess of America. It was in the town of Boston that many were imprisoned "for righteousness sake," and it is from there that the Gospel message of reformation was projected into the New World.

Not too far off from Boston is the town of Scrooby. Here we find Scrooby Manor House and the church of Scrooby which would become two of the most important spots in all of England for the founding of America. In the little town of Scrooby, the great pastor Richard Clifton led his congregation. William Brewster and William Bradford would meet with him in the manor house around the corner from the church. And there they would decide to come to the "New World", bringing with them the faith of the Separatists, the men who would later be known as the Pilgrims.

Scrooby Manor can be traced back more than a thousand years and was even written in the Domesday Book. It has also been said that it was visited by Alfred the Great, though it is hard to prove an event like this so far in the past. Some of the greatest events of all time have taken place in houses. The Scrooby Manor is a perfect example of an ancient landmark, a lived-in home, a private residence, that God has used throughout time to direct the course of history.

Today there is so much myth about the Pilgrims and Puritans, even amongst Christians, that it is important that we clear away the legend and go to the root of their story. Some people try to describe the Pilgrims as a happy, wonderful, loving, warm group of people, and the Puritans as mean ol' legalists who were always just spitting law down your throat. But this characterization is not accurate. Both the Pilgrims and the Puritans believed that God's law must be the basis of a nation's life. And both believed in being joyful and living an abundant life to the glory of their Creator.

When we study the Puritans and Pilgrims, we should remember that they were really the same people. The Pilgrims weren't even called Pilgrims until years later and were just Puritans who left the Anglican church and came to America. They were the dissenters, the non-conformists of their day. Looking back today we can see how God used both those inside and outside the established church of England to further His kingdom through true Gospel preaching.

The Puritans believed that the church of England needed to continue to reform and believed in the purification of the church. They continued the idea of Semper Reformanda, always reforming, throughout their churches and even during the persecution days of King James.

It was this time of turmoil and persecution under James which drove some of the Puritans to leave England and come to the "New World," America. These men and woman, the founders of America, would later become known as the Pilgrims through William Bradford's book, *Of Plymouth Plantation*.

Once in America, the main difference between the Pilgrims and Puritans was that the Pilgrims went to Plymouth and the Puritans went to Massachusetts Bay. Fundamentally they had the same understanding of the Word of God, the same basic theology, the same basic worldview. And they had all drunk deeply at the wells of the Reformation. They were reformed people whose life motto was 2 Corinthians 6:17:

> *Wherefore come out from among them, and be ye separate, saith the Lord, and touch not the unclean thing; and I will receive you.*

They also understood the value and importance of the law of God, not just for people and churches, but for political institutions and the governing of society. They believed that God's law was to be the basis for every nation. And they had the same end goal: to reform the Church at large and to build a Christian civilization in North America which was to be a model to the rest of the world to imitate.

The only major dissimilarities between the Puritans and the Pilgrim-Puritans were that the Pilgrims were congregational in church government and the Puritans were Episcopalian in church government. But because of the loving friendship and example of the Pilgrims towards the Puritans in Massachusetts Bay, eventually the Episcopalian Puritans also became congregationalist in their order of worship.

It is amazing to consider that of the 102 people that came over on the *Mayflower*, about fifty-two survived the first winter. And from those fifty-two who survived, there are now thirty million descendants. Incredible! But that is just what William Bradford meant when he said that they:

> . . . *cherished a great hope and inward zeal of laying good foundations, or at least making some ways toward it, for the propagation and advance of the Gospel of the kingdom of Christ in the remote parts of the world, **even though they should be but stepping stones** to others in the performance of so great a work.[emphasis added]*

The Pilgrims were ordinary men and women who took great stands for Christ, and because of their faith in God, they were enabled to begin a new and free country. They were fearless; fearless in the sense that they were willing to risk everything for what they believed Christ had called them to do. God takes ordinary men and ordinary people and uses them to change the world when they have faith that is pure and true and when their passion for the Word of God is leading and directing them.

> *We will not hide them from their children, shewing to the generation to come the praises of the LORD, and his strength, and his wonderful works that he hath done. —Psalm 78:4*

THE REFORMERS OF BUNHILL FIELDS CEMETERY

You must always be at killing sin or it will be at killing you.
—*John Owen*

To understand the history of a nation or a movement, it is important to visit its most prominent graveyards. But the greatest graveyards are not necessarily the largest, and Bunhill Fields Cemetery, the burial grounds of the non-conformists, is a prime example of this. Though relatively small in size, here rest some of the greatest men and women in the history of the sixteenth and seventeenth century.

In the Bunhill Fields Cemetery lie buried some of the great fathers of Puritanism: the authors, the theologians, the pastors, the elders and leaders of the Reformation in the seventeenth century as well as many other famous men who drew from the legacy of Puritanism. All the men buried in Bunhill Fields Cemetery were English Puritans. These were people raised up by Christ to carry the torch of reformation.

It is in Bunhill Field that we see the sarcophagus of the great John Bunyan, the "tinker of Bedford", a common man without a "formal education" who would write the single most important work of literature in the history of Christianity: *Pilgrim's Progress*.

In the history of literature there are few reformed men who have left as great an imprint on Christian literature as John Bunyan, and no one, not even Milton, has left such a powerful repository of great Christian literature as Bunyan.

Like so many men, John Bunyan started as a nobody, and then this obscure tinker changed the world. Because he was willing to accept Christ over all else, and because he was willing to set aside his foul mouth and his wild childhood, he was transformed from a double-minded man to become one of England's greatest Reformation authors.

It is also in the Bunhill Fields Cemetery that we see Susanna Wesley, mother of John Wesley, the great hymn writer Isaac Watts, author of Bible commentaries John Gill, two Cromwells as well as the son in-law to Oliver

Cromwell, and another great Christian author, Daniel Defoe, who wrote Robinson Crusoe. And it is also the resting place of John Owen, the "Prince of Puritans," buried just feet from Bunyan. These are just a few of the great men and women laid to rest in this simple cemetery after having taught the world some of the most important foundational principles of biblical Christianity, despite great sacrifice and persecution.

What an amazing thing it will be to stand in Bunhill Fields on Resurrection Day and watch the rising of so many individuals who collectively touched the lives of billions.

GROUP DISCUSSIONS AND QUESTIONS

1. How has God used one or just a few men to change history? Examples?

2. How did Christians of past eras challenge the pagan cultures in which they found themselves? How should we?

3. What did our Reformation fathers think about the importance and use of the Scriptures?

4. Genesis 50:20 says, "But as for you, you meant evil against me; but God meant it for good." Using this principle, illustrate how God used Henry VIII, a wicked ruler, to bring about significant advancements for the kingdom of God.

5. What did the weaving trade have to do with the Reformation?

6. Fill in the names: A mother trains her son; the son inspires a man; the man comes to America; and the world is changed forever.

7. What does a sounding board do? Explain it.

8. Consider our theme that God changes the world through dedicated friendships. How did Lady Willoughby's friendships affect the course of history?

9. Specifically, how did opportunities for hospitality by Lady Willoughby affect the Reformation?

10. Consider the friendships you have invested in. Are they worthwhile?

11. What is Catherine Willoughby's connection with Foxe's *Book of Martyrs*?

12. How is Boston, England responsible in part for the Puritan movement in America?

13. Name five significant men and women from Boston, England who had a powerful influence in America and explain that influence.

14. What does John Cotton, preacher in Boston, England, have to do with the founding of America?

15. How did the Reformation come to England in an unusual way? How did Reformation take hold in England?

16. Explain the three primary similarities between the Pilgrims in Plymouth and the Puritans in Massachusetts Bay.

17. What was the spiritual brotherhood?

18. Using the residents of Scrooby and 1 Corinthians 1:27-29, explain how God uses small, humble beginnings to change the world.

19. What is a "non-conformist"? Explain the importance of this.

20. Name seven significant people buried in Bunhill Fields Cemetery and give a summary of what distinguishes each one.

21. What is the reason for which the Puritans left the Church of England and came to America as Dr. Morecraft States it in A Pilgrimage to the Home of the Pilgrim Fathers?

22. What was Bunyan's trade? Why is this interesting in light of his fame?

23. What is the significance of *Pilgrim's Progress*? Have you read it?

24. Why did John Bunyan write such a lengthy preface to *Christiana*?

25. Who was John Owen? What is he known as? Describe him.

26. Describe the relationship between John Wesley and George Whitefield.

LECTURES AND VIDEO SERIES

Audio: Bunhill Fields, The Regulative Principle: How God Wants Us to Worship Him, Katherine Willoughby and Grimsthorpe Castle, Boston, A

Pilgrimage to the Home of the Pilgrim Fathers,
A Pilgrim Legacy Remembered

Video: Day 8-Bunhill Fields, Day 8-Wrap-Up, Day 9-Grimsthorpe Castle, Day 9-Boston, Day 9-Scrooby

FURTHER STUDY AND RECOMMENDED READING

Reform and Reformation England 1509-1558, by G.R. Elton

The Faithful Shepherd, by David D. Hall

The Rise of Puritanism, by William Haller

My Lady Suffolk, by Evelyn Read

A Woman of the Tudor Age, by Lady Cecilie Goff

Women, Reform, and Community in Early Modern England: Katherine Willoughby, by Melissa Franklin Harkrider

Five Generations of a Loyal Tudor House, by Lady Georgina Bertie

Famous Women of the Reformed Church, by James I. Good

Ladies of the Reformation, by J.H. Alexander

When London Burned, by G.A. Henty

Reformation and Revival, by John Brown

The Puritans: Their Origins and Successors, by D. Martin Lloyd-Jones

Family Reformation, by Scott Brown

Meet the Puritans, by Joel Beeke and Randall Pederson

John Bunyan, by John Brown

Out of the Depths, by John Newton

The Reformation: A Handbook, by T.M. Lindsay

The History of England, by Thomas Babington Macaulay

Of Plymouth Plantation, by William Bradford

Albion's Seed, by David Hackett Fischer

History of the Reformation in the 16th Century, by J.H. Merle D'Aubigne

Stories of the Reformation in Germany and England, by Rev. B. G. Johns

A Cloud of Witnesses, For the Royal Prerogatives of Jesus Christ, by John H. Thomson

Reformation Heroes, by Diana Kleyn and Joel Beeke

Dearer Than Life: A Tale of the Times of Wycliffe, by Emma Leslie

John Wycliffe, Morning Star of The Reformation (DVD)

God's Outlaw: The Story of William Tyndale (DVD)

CHAPTER XI

THE THEOLOGY OF ENGLISH ARCHITECTURE

THE MINSTER OF YORK

Every aspect of society is a reflection of the true faith and priorities of that people, and this includes architecture. One of the important elements of lifestyle we find in every country is architecture, and we see the religious perspective of the designers reflected into that architecture. In Rome we saw the Greek and Roman philosophy reflected in their temples, arches, and homes. In York we see a combination of worldview cultures in the architecture there: Saxon, Norman, Viking, and Roman—we can find it all in York. One of the most interesting monuments to architecture, representing multiple cultures over a thousand years, is the York Minster.

Five churches have stood where the present York Minster stands today. The term "Minster" itself was a Saxon word, and the first version of the church was a wooden building erected in 627 to be used for the baptism of a King Edwin of Northumbria who was marrying a Christian woman. The church was destroyed and rebuilt again and again. The present York Minster took 250 years to complete. In it we see three distinct periods of architecture.

The first architectural design is the Early English, the construction of which took place between 1220 and 1260 A.D. The north and south transepts, the area set crosswise to the nave in a cross shape, were the first part to be built and showcase the Five Sisters Window, a collection of five acutely pointed arches called lancets, each of which is fifty feet high and five feet wide. This window holds more than half-a-million pieces of glass.

The second period of architecture found in York Minster is the Decorated Gothic period, when construction continued between 1280 and 1350. The nave and the chapter house represent this time period and architectural style which uses geometric patterns in the tracery of the window and incorporates many sculptured heads above the canopies. The Great West Window, painted in 1338 and 1339, manifests this style. Also representing this era is the Tree of Jesse window, created about 1310, which shows the family tree of Christ, beginning with Jesse and including David, Solomon, Mary, and Christ himself at the top.

The third period is the Perpendicular Gothic style. This style emphasized height with flamboyant arches, a literal term for the style of arch. This arch is represented in the choir and the east end of the Minster which were built between 1361 and 1472. The Great East Window, built from 1405-1408, is the largest piece of medieval stained glass in the world. This window portrays parts of Genesis and Revelation, the beginning and the end of the world.

As we see in the stained glass windows as well as other structural elements, the architecture of the Minster was heavily influenced by the Roman Catholic church, which it was a part of for a while. Where these elements are idolatrous or violative of the Second Commandment, we must recognize them as unlawful and not imitate or copy them.

Having lasted for so many years and having played such a significant role in history of so many cultures, The Minster now stands almost hollow, with few attendees or visitors. There is a certain sadness to this fact, considering the multi-generational vision that the builders represented. They knew that the Minster would not be completed in their life time, but they knew that their children and grandchildren would benefit from their labors, and probably hoped and dreamed that their children and grandchildren would build upon their labors as well.

GRIMSTHORPE MANOR AND THE ARCHITECTURE OF THE REFORMATION

In the same way that the architecture of a city reflects the faith and priorities of the city planners and organizers, the architecture of a residence reflects faith and priorities also. This applies to landscape architecture as well as for the architecture of buildings. The England Renaissance style was heavily tempered by Protestant and Reformation thinking. Men like William of Orange and the Huguenots influenced Elizabethan and Reformation art and architecture.

The history of Grimsthorpe Castle is rich and vibrant, and so is its architectural and landscaping history. The architect and designer behind the gardens of Grimsthorpe Castle was Lancelot "Capability" Brown, England's "greatest gardener."

A simple Englishman born in 1716, Brown started as a gardener's boy and worked his way up serving under the founder of the English landscape garden, William Kent. He earned the moniker "Capability" for his own capability in work and for a characteristic comment that a client's landscape had great "capability" for improvement. He designed more than 170 gardens for some of the finest families in Great Britain.

Brown called himself a "place-maker" as opposed to a landscaper, which itself speaks to his philosophy of gardening. The previous popular style of gardening had been the very formal geometric manner, most well-known in the gardens of Versailles. Brown rejected this style, and instead worked with the natural ebb and flow of the English landscape. He is credited with saying, "Nature abhors a straight line." He has been both admired and criticized for imitating nature. But in the end, what is clear is that he appreciated the beauty and order he saw in nature, and tried, to the best of his ability, to bring formal, contrived, English landscape back to that originally created beauty and flow.

The three thousand acres of park at Grimsthorpe include lakes, woods, and rolling pastures that were all designed by Brown. His design of "gardenless" gardens did away with the previous structured, forced patterns and left large fields of smooth grass running straight up to the house, with scattered trees and lakes about. While Lancelot Capability Brown's statement of faith is unclear today, he was heavily influenced by Reformation ideas of the time and helped England to move away from the French Rococo styles which were so popular. His message of landscape is clear: What was created originally is beautiful and should be cherished and cultivated and enjoyed.

CATHOLIC ARCHITECTURE TORN DOWN BY THE REFORMATION

During the Reformation, as more and more people began to see the problems with Catholicism and all the trappings that accompanied it, they began to realize that "the high places" had to be torn down. An interesting example of this happened to the cathedral in St. Andrews, Scotland. The remains of the cathedral that we can see today on the cliffs of the beautiful town of St. Andrews have been there since the common folk listened to the teaching of John Knox hundreds of years ago and tore the catholic church to pieces. The destruction of the church was not the result he intended, but the people were so fired up by his Biblical teaching that their response was to take the Scripture at its word and tear down the idols, tear down the temples, tear down the high places that had any association with false teaching or idolatry.

In many respects, the cathedral of St. Andrews is a torn-down version of York Minster. Today we can still see that it was designed in Romanesque style, though we do see a mixture of Gothic in with it since it was built in the twelfth century. We can also still see the cross layout in the basilica style with transepts, and naves for the isle. But today that is all that is left of the church at St. Andrews.

The destruction of the monasteries and stained glass windows of the cathedrals and the Catholic idols has been considered tragic and disgraceful by many today. But when it comes to the worship of God, only what He commands is permitted. In many ways, the torn remains of the broken church are a much better way to symbolize and remember the paganism than it would have been to have left it intact.

When we look at the Scriptures, we repeatedly see the reference to the tearing down of high places and the honoring of God in their destruction. Here are just a few of the verses that the Reformers of the sixteenth and seventeenth century made foundational in their teaching:

> *And I will destroy your high places, and cut down your images, and cast your carcasses upon the carcasses of your idols, and my soul shall abhor you. —Leviticus 26:30*

> *Then ye shall drive out all the inhabitants of the land from before you, and destroy all their pictures, and destroy all their molten images, and quite pluck down all their high places. —Numbers 33:52*

> *Ye shall utterly destroy all the places, wherein the nations which ye shall possess served their gods, upon the high mountains, and upon the hills, and under every green tree. —Deuteronomy 12:2*

> *Happy art thou, O Israel: who is like unto thee, O people saved by the LORD, the shield of thy help, and who is the sword of thy excellency! and thine enemies shall be found liars unto thee; and thou shalt tread upon their high places. —Deuteronomy 33:29*

> *Zebulun and Naphtali were a people that jeoparded their lives unto the death in the high places of the field. —Judges 5:18*

The Reformation came, and it stayed. Ultimately if you tear down an idol and destroy it, there is no risk of it being rebuilt or of the people returning to it.

GROUP DISCUSSIONS AND QUESTIONS

1. How does landscape factor into the architectural theology of the castle at Grimsthorpe?

2. What does Adam's first mission in the Garden have to do with

Grimsthorpe's landscape?

3. Who was Lancelot Capability Brown and what was his influence?

4. Compare and contrast the architecture and its theological message of the York Minster and the Scrooby church, both a thousand years old.

5. Define "minster" and give the origins of the name.

6. The York Minster is thought to have been built on what original Roman building?

7. How long did it take to complete the York Minster? What does that tell you about multigenerational commitment to architectural and cultural objectives?

8. In what way does this great cathedral of York demonstrate Roman Catholic syncretism?

9. What feeling does perpendicular Gothic architecture create?

10. Explain what mullions and transoms are.

11. Where did the name "shambles" come from? Describe some of the peculiarities of this rambling street.

12. Why was a cemetery or graveyard a priority in the architectural planning of a church?

13. Define these architectural terms: basilica, trancepts, naves, aisle.

14. Why do we want to "tear down the high places"?

LECTURES AND VIDEO SERIES

Audio: York and the Statue of Constantine, Catherine Willoughby and Grimsthorpe Castle, St. Andrews

Video: Day 9-Grimsthorpe, Day 10-Welcome to York, Day 10-York Minster, Day 10-The Walls of York, Day 10-Wrap-Up, Day 11-Welcome to St. Andrews

FURTHER STUDY AND RECOMMENDED READING

History of the Reformation in Europe in the Time of Calvin, by J.H. Merle D'Aubigne

Life in a Medieval Castle, by Frances and Joseph Gies

The History of England, by Thomas Babington Macaulay

Architecture: Form, Space & Order, by Francis D. K. Ching

A History of Architecture on the Comparative Method, by Sir Banister Fletcher

The Castellated and Domestic Architecture of Scotland, by David and Ross MacGibbon,

The Classical Language of Architecture, by John Summerson

A History of Scottish Architecture From the Renaissance to the Present Day, by Miles Glendinning, Ranald MacInnes, Aonghus MacKechnie,

De Architectura, by Vitruvius

CHAPTER XII

SPURGEON:
THE LAST GREAT PURITAN

On January 6, 1850, at age fifteen, Charles Haddon Spurgeon walked into a church, heard the Gospel and professed faith in Christ, but his conversion was not just a feeling on the inside of him. The message of Christ and truth had deeply affected him and he was fundamentally changed for life. He was baptized in May and preached his first sermon in the winter of that same year. Within three years, he was working as a pastor of a small church in Cambridgeshire and had published a Gospel tract. This is the story of a young man who was passionate after God and became the prince of preachers.

To this day, Spurgeon has had more sermons published than any man in all of the history of the church. He is probably also the most quoted preacher of all time. His sermons have continued to influence people since his death in the 1890s.

In some respects, Spurgeon represents the high water mark of Reformed and Baptistic teaching. Certainly in the nineteenth century, this was true. But he did not stand in a vacuum; he looked to the predecessors, to the men that came before him, men like John Calvin and Dr. John Gill.

Today people don't understand what a ferocious defender of the fundamentals of Christian orthodoxy he was, especially when it came to issues like the sovereignty of God. He was without peer in his time. As he would give his sermons, they would be transcribed and then sold for a penny a piece and read everywhere. This changed the world. Many people came to Christ under the ministry of Charles Spurgeon.

Spurgeon was a great fan of John Calvin and a great defender of the reformers. He was a man who was a defender of the concepts of Reformation worship. And though he may not have had the precise terminology that was used in other circles, he preached against the Catholic liturgical holidays and preached for the Scripture to be the foundation for all the decision-making.

He started as a young man who was promoted by the Lord at an early age through men recognizing his God-given talents and gifts. His maxim-verse as he began his career was, "Let no man despise thy youth" (I Timothy 4:12). This is a lesson for us today: We should never despise the work of the Lord in young men. You never know what the Lord can do.

But you have to be a special young man if you are going to rise to the kind of leadership of Spurgeon. Throughout his life, he was known as the great preacher of the doctrines of grace and of the sovereignty of God. It was recognized that he had an unusual gift to be able to speak in the scriptural language of poetry, through careful exegesis of the Scripture. He communicated in a language that everyone understood using the principles and style that we see the Lord using in his parables.

More than anything, Spurgeon preached Christ. Everything he did was about the Lord Jesus Christ. This was so overwhelmingly visible throughout his life that people understood that behind the structure, behind the explanation of the law, there was always the heart for his Savior.

Throughout his life, Spurgeon showed that the Gospel of Christ, successfully preached in the vein of his Reformation forefathers. Though he was as ridiculed and slandered as his spiritual forebears had been, the Holy Spirit continued to rout his enemies, as he had done those in the past.

But how soon we forget. Within fifty years of Spurgeon's death, his congregation, formerly made up of hundreds, had dwindled to dozens. We must always remember to tell the stories and to continue the legacies of the great men of the past. For generations, Spurgeon's legacy and message was lost.

Thankfully for the kingdom, over the past forty years there has been a revival of appreciation of Charles Spurgeon that has led to a transformation in pulpits all over the world. And there has been a revival in the preaching of the sovereign grace of God. We must not forget reformers like Charles Spurgeon and the legacy he left us. We must tell their stories.

Spurgeon said:

> If Christ is not all to you He is nothing to you. He will never go into partnership as a part Saviour of men. If He be something He must be everything, and if He be not everything He is nothing to you. — Charles Spurgeon

> You need to read. Renounce as much as you will all light literature, but study as much as possible sound theological works, especially the Puritan writers, and expositions of the Bible. . . , the best way for you to spend your leisure is to be either reading or praying. —Charles Spurgeon

GROUP DISCUSSIONS AND QUESTIONS

1. What practical method was used to disseminate the Gospel and doctrine during the late 1800s?

2. Why is Spurgeon called the Prince of Preachers?

3. How does 1 Timothy 4:12 apply to Spurgeon?

4. What does the architecture of the Metropolitan Tabernacle say about the emphasis of the preaching there?

5. What was distinctive about Spurgeon's style of speaking and teaching and how did he come by this style? What does your style of speaking reflect?

LECTURES AND VIDEO SERIES

Audio: The Metropolitan Tabernacle

Video: Day 8-The Metropolitan Tabernacle

FURTHER STUDY AND RECOMMENDED READING

Morning and Evening, by Charles Spurgeon

The Forgotten Spurgeon, by Iain Murray

The Soul Winner, by Charles Spurgeon

Eccentric Preachers, by Charles Spurgeon

Family Reformation, by Scott Brown

Spurgeon Gold, by Ray Comfort

PART IV
SCOTLAND TO
AMERICA

CHAPTER XIII

THE ORIGINS OF SCOTLAND/ALBA

INTRODUCTION

There are very few national histories that should inspire Christians as much as the story of Scotland. Our own America itself is inextricably linked to the story of Scotland. Many of our first settlers, the great men of our founding era, including preachers, theologians, and missionaries, came from the shores of Scotland. America certainly inherited more than simply the men of Scotland. We inherited the ideas of Scotland.

These inherited ideas include principles of freedom, common law, and a vast repository of theological wisdom which was birthed through some of the most difficult times in the church, the times of the Scots Covenanters and the "Killing Times." These ideas, stories, and examples of manhood in Scotland go back thousands of years all the way to its origins. Because, in large part, our own experience as Americans was birthed by the Scots, it is important that we start at the beginning and ask ourselves the question:

Where did the Scottish people come from?

THEORIES ABOUT THE ORIGINS OF THE SCOTS IN SCOTLAND

There are many different theories about the origin of the Scots. One helpful place we can start to study these theories is with an important document called the Declaration of Arbroath. A few years after the Battle of Bannockburn in 1314, the Scottish nobles wrote an open letter to the Pope declaring the freedom of Scotland. This declaration also laid out a short history of the Scots going back to the time of the apostles, stating that:

> ...among other famous nations our own, the Scots, has been graced
> with widespread renown. They journeyed from Greater Scythia by
> way of the Tyrrhenian Sea and the Pillars of Hercules, and dwelt
> for a long course of time in Spain among the most savage tribes, but
> nowhere could they be subdued by any race, however barbarous.
> Thence they came, twelve hundred years after the people of Israel
> crossed the Red Sea, to their home in the west where they still
> live today. The Britons they first drove out, the Picts they utterly
> destroyed, and, even though very often assailed by the Norwegians,
> the Danes and the English, they took possession of that home with
> many victories and untold efforts; and, as the historians of old time
> bear witness, they have held it free of all bondage ever since. In their
> kingdom there have reigned one hundred and thirteen kings of their
> own royal stock, the line unbroken [by] a single foreigner.

Sixteenth-century historian Raphael Holinshed, the source for a number of William Shakespeare's plays, appears to corroborate and expound upon the history given at Arbroath in his unfinished work, The Chronicles of England, Scotland, and Ireland. His account describes the legendary figure Gathelus, the son of a king in Greece, who was banished and journeyed to Egypt with a ship full of friends. For a time, he worked as a mercenary for the Pharaoh. After eliminating Pharaoh's enemies, he won the hand of the Pharaoh's daughter, Scota, after whom Gathelus would name his people.

According to this version of the legend, Gathelus and his wife Scota knew Moses. When Pharaoh began to mistreat the Israelites, Gathelus gathered a fleet and left Egypt with all his tribe. They arrived in Spain, only to end up continually warring with the people there. Wishing to end the wars and hearing of a green island in the sea, Gathelus and his sons, Hiberus and Himecus, moved the Scots from Spain to what they named Hibernia, the Latin name for Ireland, presumably named for Hiberus. A few hundred years later, a prince of these "scotishmen" found the Scottish Hebrides to be good for cattle, and moved a number of Scot families to the top of north Britain. Just as the south became known as the land of the Angles or England, so the north became the land of the Scots and henceforth Scotland.

Though many would cast aside or ridicule the story of Gathelus, the Greek-Egyptian-Spaniard-Irish-Scot, it is important to remember that these "legends" were upheld for hundreds of years by men like Robert the Bruce, Sir Walter Scott, and Raphael Holinshed. Note that Holinshed was Shakespeare's historical resource when writing *Macbeth*, *King Lear*, and *Cymbeline*.

SCOTTISH PAGANISM AND ST. ANDREW

According to other Scottish legends, the apostle Andrew came to Scotland during the early days after Christ's death and resurrection, preaching Christ to the lost. At this time Scotland was full of barbarian Picts and Scottish pagans. Andrew is said to have turned Scotland from a vile, pagan land into a country brimming with openness to the Gospel and Christ. In the Declaration of Arbroath the Scottish lords say that:

> ...the King of kings and Lord of lords, our Lord Jesus Christ, after His Passion and Resurrection, called them [the Scots], even though settled in the uttermost parts of the earth, almost the first to His most holy faith. Nor would He have them confirmed in that faith by merely anyone but by the first of His Apostles—by calling, though second or third in rank—the most gentle Saint Andrew, the Blessed Peter's brother, and desired him to keep them under his protection as their patron forever.

While it is very hard, if not impossible, to verify either of these two legends, and while there is controversy surrounding the true origin of the Scottish people, there is reason to believe that there is a very early origin of the Scots and that there was a strong influence of Christianity during the first two centuries. This could have included the missionary work of Andrew himself, hence the flag of Scotland, the Saltire, known as St. Andrew's Cross, reportedly first flown at the Battle of Bannockburn, as well as the naming of St. Andrew's town and castle, and an entire nation's history built around the stories handed down generation to generation of the missionary work of Andrew.

Whatever the case may be as to Andrew having visited Scotland, J. H. Merle D'Aubigne, said:

> It is certain that the tidings of the Son of Man, crucified and raised again during the reign of Emperor Tiberius, later spread through these islands more rapidly than the dominion of the emperors, and that before the end of the second century, many churches worshipped Christ beyond the walls of Hadrian.

THE ROMAN SETTLEMENTS OF SCOTLAND

Whenever these early tribes did get to Scotland, they found the Picts and the Britons to also be inhabiting this little island that was constantly brimming with war. These three groups, the Scots, Picts, and Britons, were perpetually fighting each other or teaming up and taking turns killing each other off.

In 55 B.C., the Romans arrived in Britain fully prepared to "come, see, and conquer", but it wasn't quite that simple. It took more than a hundred years after Caesar had first come to Britain for General Agricola in 80 A.D. to finally march into lower Scotland. There were many little skirmishes in the never-ending feud between the conquerors and the unconquered. Eventually, in the gigantic battle of Mons Graupius, ten thousand Caledonians were slaughtered, and the rest fled to the Highlands. Agricola finally returned to Rome, but the Scots, though wounded, remained unconquered.

The Romans could not hold the forts that Agricola had set against the Scots who continued their fierce and relentless resistance against the invaders. About 123 AD, Emperor Hadrian came to Britain and built a wall from the River Tyne to Solway, about 73 miles long. Twenty years later, Emperor Antoninus Pius began work on the Antonine wall, about a hundred miles north of Hadrian's wall. The Scots continued breaking through or climbing over the Roman walls. In 208 AD, Emperor Septimus Severus decided to end Caledonian rebellions for good. He marched straight through Scotland, repaired Hadrian's wall building roads and bridges. The Scottish resistance persisted. Finally, Severus simply repaired the wall built by Hadrian and died in York. By 400 AD, the Romans left Briton and Caledonia for good.

But the Romans had unintentionally been a blessing for Briton. With the Roman armies, came Roman towns and with these came households which often included Christian members. Just one example of this is the Missionary Patrick who was born in Roman Briton to a leading household. He was enslaved, became saved, escaped, and then went back to the Irish, his former masters, as a missionary.

GROUP DISCUSSIONS AND QUESTIONS

1. How is our history in America connected to the history in Scotland?

2. What is the significance of the Declaration of Arbroath?

3. Who was Ralph Holinshed and why does it matter?

4. Why was St. Andrews a place of pilgrimage for the Roman Catholics?

5. Explain the connection between the Pharaoh in Egypt and Scottish history.

6. How long before the birth of Christ do we think the first Romans came to Britain?

7. From what Roman general does comes our word "agriculture"?

8. Who built Hadrian's wall?

9. Who was the last Roman to try to conquer Britain?

FURTHER STUDY AND RECOMMENDED READING

The Chronicles of England, Scotland, and Ireland, by Raphael Holinshed

History of the Reformation of the Sixteenth Century, by J.H. Merle D'Aubigne

The Declaration of Arbroath, 1320: The Scottish Nobles

How the Scots Invented the Modern World, by Arthur Herman

How the Scots Saved Christendom: Tales of Bravehearts and Covenanters, by Vision Forum (CD)

CHAPTER XIV

THE EMERGENCE OF A SCOTTISH CHURCH

COLUMBA AND THE ISLAND OF IONA

It is interesting to note that many of the Scots viewed themselves as a nation set-apart to the Lord. In the Declaration of Arbroath, they stated that they were chosen "almost the first to His most holy faith," meaning that they had known the truth of Christ since the early days of their existence in northern Briton.

In 563 A.D., a man named Columba sailed with twelve friends from Ireland to Scotland with the hope of continuing the Christianization of the Scots. They arrived at the island Hy, which was given to them and renamed Iona. Columba established Iona as a haven for Christianity and built houses and a church. Iona became a specifically Christian island with almost all the Scots near to Iona turning to Christ. Columba lived for thirty-four years among the Scots, traveling all around, preaching Christ. He also copied the Psalms and many other parts of the Bible. When he died, he was buried on

Iona, but he is said to have been removed and buried beside Patrick in the County Down, Ireland. Dr. Joe Morecraft wrote that:

> By his death, Columba's achievements were monumental. This servant of God established several abbeys and mission outposts in Ireland and northern Britain, one of the most important of which was the Christian center and school of theology on the isle of Iona, or Icolmkill, in A.D. 563. Iona is three miles long and one mile wide, a rocky and windswept island off the southwest coast of the island of Mull, which is located off the southwest coast of Scotland.

Why did Columba choose this remote and bare island for his Christian center? It may have been self-exile because of guilt, as he was the cause of a great battle in 561 between Diarmait, King of Ireland, and Columba's relatives, the Clan Neil at Culdreimhne (now Cooladrummon). Allegedly, Columba mustered the Clan Neil for the war for the purpose of avenging two grievances against King Diarmait. One grievance was that Diarmait had slain Columba's clansman, the young Prince Curnan, who had taken sanctuary with him after having caused the death of a playfellow during the sports at Tara. The other was a decision which Columba considered unjust given against him by Diarmait in the matter of the ownership of a book.

Whatever the reason, in God's providence Iona was the means for beginning the true Christianization of Scotland. If Columba had not come to Iona from Ireland, Scotland would surely have had a very different history than we know today. Iona laid the foundation for every great event of Scottish history to come in the next 1400 years.

But Columba wasn't just another priest run off to the missions. He believed in many of the principles which we see exemplified in the Reformation. J. H. Merle D'Aubigne says that:

> It was the Holy Ghost, Columba maintained, that made a servant of God. When the youth of Caledonia assembled around the elders on these savage shores, or in their humble chapel, these ministers of the Lord would say to them: "The Holy Scriptures are the only

*rule of faith. Throw aside all merit of works, and look for salvation
to the grace of God alone. Beware of a religion which consists of
outward observances: it is better to keep your heart pure before God
than to abstain from meats. One alone is your head, Jesus Christ.
Bishops and presbyters are equal; they should be the husbands of
one wife, and have their children in subjection. [Emphasis added]*

This is very different from what we see later in the theology of the Church of
Rome, or even in later centuries on Iona. This is the theology of a pure-minded
seeker after God. Columba truly yearned to make disciples of nations and to
continue sanctifying himself at the same time. D'Aubigne goes on to explain:

*Although subject to the same passions as ourselves, he wrestled
against his weakness, and would not have one moment lost for the
glory of God. He prayed and read, he wrote and taught, he preached
and redeemed the time. With indefatigable activity he went from
house to house, and from kingdom to kingdom. The king of the Picts
was converted as were many of his people; precious manuscripts
were conveyed to Iona; a school of theology was founded there, in
which the Word was studied; and many received through faith the
salvation which is in Christ Jesus. [Emphasis added]*

THE LAW OF THE INNOCENTS AND THE COLUMBA-DISCIPLED CULDEES

Columba's missionary outpost on Iona fanned the flames of Christianity in
Scotland. Columba didn't just bring some idea of "meek Christianity", his
yearning to return to the law of God drove him to concepts like The Law of
the Innocents which his follower and biographer Adomnán would promulgate.
"Columba brought Christ, and with Christ came Christian culture." The Law
of the Innocents said things like: "… he who from this day forward shall put a
woman to death and does not do penance according to the Law, shall not only
perish in eternity, and be cursed for God and Adomnán."

Columba had turned Iona into a place that was actively taking stands
on important issues of the day, such as the rising tyranny of the "Bishop of

Rome." Out of this came the Culdees, a sect dating back to the early days of Celtic Christianity in Scotland. The growth of the Culdee/reformed church of Christ and truth can be attributed in large part to Columba's influence in Scotland. During the days when the church of Rome was once again taking over Iona and Scotland, it was the Culdees, a Celtic word meaning worshippers of God, who would preserve the simple Gospel message for centuries in providential preparation of a great reformation of Church and state to take place a thousand years after Columba.

THE TAKEOVER OF ROMAN CATHOLICISM

In the 7th century, the British-Celtic church was being forced back into submission to the Roman Pope by intimidation and force. The Roman Church was getting nervous about the goings on out in the backwoods of Scotland, and they began to take a much stronger hold on both Scotland and Briton. Dr. Joe Morecraft states:

> At one point in their history, most of twelve hundred unarmed British Christians were slaughtered by the Anglo-Saxon king Aethelfrith and his army, after which they burned a leading center of British Christianity, probably at the instigation of Rome. Iona held out for a long time, being "the last citadel of liberty in the western world, and popery was filled with anger at that miserable band which in its remote corner refused to bend before it.

By the time the eighth century rolled around, the leaders of places like Iona had become Romanized once again. But the battle for truth wasn't over. Some continued in the Culdee tradition of honoring God simply as the Scriptures commanded. This was a theological battle to continue into the sixteenth and seventeenth century. Morecraft also notes:

> It was upon the work of these "Culdees" . . . that the Wycliffite Lollards built much of their ministry in the fourteenth century and beyond. It was these Lollards that God used to pave the way for the Scottish Reformation in the sixteenth century.

Rome may have taken back Iona, but the witness of the Culdees was never extinguished, and their testimony would later help pave the way for the future Reformation in Europe.

GROUP DISCUSSIONS AND QUESTIONS

1. What is the significance of Iona?

2. What is Columba's legacy to us today?

3. Who succeeded Columba and what important literary work did he leave?

4. Why is the protection of the innocent an important biblical principle for every nation to understand?

5. Why was it important to the church of Rome to abolish the opposition at Iona?

6. What important early Celtic group was significantly impacted by Columba?

7. Was the early reformed view, held to by many fifth and sixth century Scots, wiped out by the Church of Rome? Discuss the theology of the perseverance of the saints.

8. By the early eighth century, many of the uncompromising Celtic and Scottish Christians were saddened by the backsliding of the Celtic church in subservience to the Roman church. How did God use this to help birth the Reformation of the sixteenth century?

LECTURES

Audio: The Culdees

FURTHER STUDY AND RECOMMENDED READING :

The Law of the Innocents, by Adomnán of Iona

Vita Columbae, by Adomnán of Iona

History of the Reformation of the Sixteenth Century, by J. H. Merle D'Aubigne

Journey to the End of Iona, A Reformation Pilgrimage to Iona, by Doug Phillips

Iona's Gospel Light; The Global Advancement of Christ's Kingdom, by Dr. Joseph Morecraft [8/6/08]

www.visionforumministries.org/issues/news_and_reports/ionas_Gospel_light.aspx

www.visionforumministries.org/issues/news_and_reports/journey_to_the_end_of_the_eart.aspx#n2

Life in a Medieval Village, by Frances and Joseph Gies

Life in a Medieval Castle, by Frances and Joseph Gies

The Story of the Scottish Church, by Thomas McCrie

CHAPTER XV

HOW FREEDOM-LOVING MEN SHAPED A CULTURE

THE ORIGIN OF THE SCOTTISH AND ENGLISH WAR

King Alexander III of Scotland died on March 19, 1286, leaving no heir and only a young granddaughter, Margaret, by his daughter and the Prince of Norway. G. A. Henty stated:

> The hopes of the country now rested on the 'maid of Norway,' who alone stood between the throne and a number of claimants, most of whom would be prepared to support their claims, and thus bring unnumbered woes upon Scotland. Most unhappily for the country, the maid died on her voyage to Scotland. The succession therefore became open.

It was at this time that Edward I, King of England, or "Longshanks" as he was called, began angling for control in Scotland. This had started as a treaty for marriage between his son and Margaret, but when the maid died, he openly declared himself "Lord-Paramount of Scotland" and called upon every Scotsman to do homage and acknowledge Edward as their rightful lord. Edward rapidly gained the epithet, "Hammer of the Scots," and he deserved it. On November 17, 1292 Edward appointed John Baliol, one of the weaker claimants for the Scottish throne, as his puppet-king.

WILLIAM WALLACE AND THE CAUSE OF SCOTTISH INDEPENDENCE

One of the few men who openly opposed the takeover of Edward was Sir Malcolm Wallace. Wallace was a knight and a landowner giving him a position of some nobility. When he and his eldest son refused to swear allegiance to the Edward, they were forced into hiding and eventually murdered by Sir John Fenwick and his English soldiers.

Wallace's young son William was not killed with his father and elder brother, and he never forgot their brutal deaths. He was only eighteen when he is said to have had his first encounter with the English. After he had been fishing one day, some soldiers in the train of Earl Percy, governor of Ayr, marched by and commanded Wallace to hand over the fish he had caught. Henty says:

> [Wallace] replied that they were welcome to half of them. Not satisfied with this, they seized the basket and prepared to carry it off. Wallace resisted, and one of them drew his sword. Wallace seized the staff of his net and struck his opponent's sword from his hand; this he snatched up and stood on guard, while the other four rushed upon him. Wallace smote the first so terrible a blow that his head was cloven from skull to collarbone; with the next blow he severed the right arm of another, and then disabled a third.

The two remaining soldiers ran back to the earl asking for help, but when he found that it was one man who they had confronted, he stated that he would do nothing as, in this instance, he had more respect for the action of the lone fisherman than his own men.

At this age Wallace was already described as being of "great stature and strength", and though naturally courteous and gentle in his personality, he was not the sort of person to put up with funny business. He was also very well-trained in both arms and languages. By this time, Wallace was outlawed by the English for another run-in he had when he killed Selbye, the son of the governor of Dundee, in self defense. At this point, Wallace found harbor with his uncles, Sir Ronald Crawford and then his uncle, Sir Richard Wallace of Riccarton. During his stay with them, he gathered "a party of young men, eager spirits like himself, and swore perpetual hostility to the English."

Within Scotland the name of Wallace was becoming synonymous with heroic defense of freedom and a hatred for English tyranny. Wallace, though not a reformed man by any means, had taken the principles laid out by men like Columba and Adomnán and applied them to his beliefs and principles, causing him to be ever working to defend and help the Scottish families sore oppressed by the English soldiers. Wallace counted the cost and chose freedom and the rough life of an outlaw instead of the comfortable, complacent life embraced by many Scottish lords who blindly swore allegiance to England and died as miserable, uninspired men.

Some of the events in Wallace's life were larger than life, just like his reputation. At one point, Wallace was imprisoned and doomed to hang, but became so sick in prison that he appeared to be dead, was carried out to be buried, but managed an extraordinary recovery and faked a funeral to cover his escape.

As his reputation grew, so his band grew from a local outlaw band to a small military force, finally becoming an organized rebellion against the English. Henty said that Wallace:

> ...introduced an organization among those who were found to be friendly to the cause, and by bugle notes taken up and repeated from spot to spot orders could be despatched over a wide extent of country, by which the members of his band knew whether to assemble or disperse, to prepare to attack an enemy, or to retire to their fastnesses.

One of the first real battles for Wallace's rebel army took place against John Fenwick, the man who had killed his father, and two hundred soldiers marching to Ayr. Wallace had only fifty men with him, but took the victory after killing about half the English, including Fenwick, and sent the rest fleeing. He also captured the convoy, provisions, and two hundred horses.

For a designated two months, Wallace and the English held to a truce, but it was hard for him to stay inactive and out of sight, and he continued his adventures during this time. As soon as the two months were up, however, Wallace immediately attacked the English. In return, the English brought a force of 1000 men against Wallace, who only had fifty. Wallace promptly killed the two officers in command and a total of 120 English were killed, more than twenty by Wallace himself before he drew off his Scots. Wallace was clearly leading Scotland.

Some time during his escapades, Wallace had secretly wed Marion Braidfute of Lanark. One day in mid- 1297, Wallace was in Lanark and for some reason or another became engaged in a fray in the streets. The leader of the English soldiers was Hazelrig, the son of the governor of the town. As the fray passed Marion's house, she drew in Wallace and his small band before they could be finished off by the English. They escaped through the back door, but no sooner had they gone, then the English broke in and brutally killed Marion. That very evening Wallace returned, sacked Lanark and killed Hazelrig. Henty says that it was around this time that:

> Proclamations were immediately made out in the name of Wallace, and were sent off by mounted messengers throughout the country. In these he announced to the people of Scotland that he had raised the national banner and had commenced a war for the freeing of the country from the English, and that as a first step he had captured Lanark. He called upon all true Scotchmen to rally. . . .

Christ is always in the business of preparing men to help guide his providential timeline. Wallace was one such man. Sadly, as every great leader, he suffered tremendous personal loss and betrayal in return for his heroic defense of Scotland.

One of the great gifts of God that goes into truly great leaders is a passionate commitment to truth, born out of faith in what they believe and true courage. In the film immortalizing Wallace's life, *Braveheart*, director Mel Gibson portrays Wallace saying "Men follow courage..." This is an important point which Wallace, in real life, understood. God has designed men to respond to masculine and courageous leadership. This is why the men of Scotland followed Wallace, and this is why Wallace has forever been memorialized as a hero in freedom's cause. Through his courageous leadership, Wallace inspired the common folk and emboldened the nobles.

Though not a perfect man, William Wallace exhibited the spirit of a true reformer, yearning to lead his country away from bondage. He was specifically used of God to further the knowledge of truth and freedom, paving the way for men like John Knox hundreds of years later.

In the end, Wallace was willing to pay the full price rather than give in to a tyrant or go back on his country. Sometime in 1305, Wallace was betrayed to the English. On August 23, during his one-day mock trial, condemnation, and execution, he argued to the end that as a native Scot he never had sworn fealty or allegiance to Edward and that he was completely justified in fighting for the freedom of his country. William Wallace was executed in London on August 23, 1305. Mutilated, cut up while yet living, Wallace died at the age of thirty-two. John Joseph Lalor in his *Cyclopedia of Political Science, Political Economy, and of the Political History of the United States, Vol. 3* says:

> *After defending his country with heroism for several years, Wallace was betrayed into the hands of Edward, who caused him to be executed in London in 1305. His head was placed on London bridge, and a quarter of his body exposed at New Castle, Berwick, Stirling and Perth, respectively. These bloody trophies, far from frightening the Scots into submission, aroused their wrath and strengthened their courage.*

Henty, an Englishman, observed:

> *Every cruelty attended his execution. He was drawn through*

the streets at the tails of horses; he was hung for some time by a halter, but was taken down while yet alive; he was mutilated and disembowelled, his head then cut off, his body divided in four, his head impaled over London Bridge, and his quarters distributed to four principal towns in Scotland.

God raised up Wallace, laying the foundation for freedom which would be needed for the Reformation and the birth of America. Wallace understood that this wasn't about his personal goals. He understood that he was fighting for the future generations of Scotland and the world.

A nobler character than Wallace is not to be found in history. Alone, a poor and landless knight, by his personal valour and energy he aroused the spirit of his countrymen, and in spite of the opposition of the whole of the nobles of his country banded the people in resistance against England, and for a time wrested all Scotland from the hands of Edward. His bitter enemies the English were unable to adduce any proofs that the epithets of ferocious and bloodthirsty, with which they were so fond of endowing him, had even a shadow of foundation, and we may rather believe the Scotch accounts that his gentleness and nobility of soul were equal to his valour. Of his moderation and wisdom when acting as governor of Scotland there can be no doubt, while the brilliant strategy which first won the battle of Stirling, and would have gained that of Falkirk had not the treachery and cowardice of the cavalry ruined his plans, show that under other circumstances he would have taken rank as one of the greatest commanders of his own or any age. —G.A. Henty

ROBERT THE BRUCE AND THE DEATH OF EDWARD I

Part of true leadership is seeing things that other people don't see, and, when others are ready to quit, persevering with purpose and resolve. This is the story of Wallace, and it would become the story of Robert Bruce. After the murder of Wallace, Bruce picked up the mantle of leadership in Scotland

and began to act with responsibility and courage. During the early days of Wallace, Bruce had wavered on whether he should side with the English or not, but at the time of Wallace's death, it was clear whose side he was on.

In the beginning of 1306, Robert Bruce left King Edward's court to take up the defense of Scotland. At the age of thirty-two, he like Wallace was a young man in a position of great leadership in Scotland. In the Declaration of Arbroath, written in 1320, Bruce is described as a:

> *...most tireless Prince, King and Lord, the Lord Robert. He, that his people and his heritage might be delivered out of the hands of our enemies, met toil and fatigue, hunger and peril, like another Macabaeus or Joshua and bore them cheerfully. Him, too, divine providence, his right of succession according to or laws and customs which we shall maintain to the death, and the due consent and assent of us all have made our Prince and King. To him, as to the man by whom salvation has been wrought unto our people, we are bound both by law and by his merits that our freedom may be still maintained, and by him, come what may, we mean to stand.*

The tidings rapidly spread across Scotland that Bruce was going against the English, and Scotland breathed a sigh of relief. On the 25th of March, 1306, Bruce was crowned king in the Chapel Royal of Scone. And the great banner of the kings of Scotland was planted behind the throne once again. At first, Bruce was not as successful against the English as Wallace had been. But he continued to persevere against the English, and in the end, it paid off.

Edward stormed at the news of Bruce's rebellion and determined to send an invasion on Scotland which would end Scottish resistance once and for all. All of England's great fighting power was called into the cause. Edward, sick and worn out, made his men promise that they would carry him along with the army until Scotland was subdued. He died, however, just outside of Scotland, on July 7, 1307.

Upon his father's death, Edward II took over the command of the Scottish invasion, but he was not the man his father was, and it proved a favorable turning point in the destiny of Scotland.

THE BATTLE OF BANNOCKBURN

It was on June 24, 1314, that one of the greatest events in Scottish history, the Battle of Bannockburn began. This would become the most decisive battle in the war for Scottish independence. Edward II had come to Scotland with the preliminary aim of relieving Stirling Castle. The real purpose, however, was to find and destroy the Scottish army in the field, and thus end the war.

Though it is not known for sure how many men fought at Bannockburn, traditional estimates have placed the English infantry at about 10,000 men, though Edward was known to have mustered around 21,000. It is probable that only half of the English army actually was at the Battle of Bannockburn. The estimate for the Scottish army has been around 6,000 infantry. The odds were truly against the Scots, showing us just how important this victory really was for the Scottish cause.

Bruce was awaiting the arrival of the English south of Stirling near the Bannock Burn in Scotland. And it is said that Bruce was flying the Saltire flag, or the St. Andrew's cross of Scotland, as the Scots went into battle. Bruce's army, like Wallace's before him, was mainly made up of infantry with long spears. The Scots also had about 500 archers which helped to balance out the army. On the first day of the battle, Sunday the 23rd, there occurred one of the greatest and most memorable stories of the battle. As Henty recounts it:

> In front of the ranks of the defenders the king [Bruce] was riding upon a small palfrey, not having as yet put on his armour for the battle. On his helmet he wore a purple cap surmounted by a crown. Seeing him thus within easy reach, Sir Henry de Bohun, cousin of the Earl of Hereford, laid his lance in rest and spurred down upon the king. Bruce could have retired within the lines of his soldiers; but confident in his own prowess, and judging how great an effect a success under such circumstances would have upon the spirits of his troops, he spurred forward to meet his assailant armed only with his axe. As the English knight came thundering down, the king touched his palfrey with his spur, and the horse, carrying but a light weight, swerved quickly aside; De Bohun's lance missed his stroke, and before

he had time to draw rein or sword, the king, standing up in his stirrups, dealt him so tremendous a blow with his axe as he passed, that it cleft through helmet and brain, and the knight fell dead to the ground.

The Scots charged forward with a shout and drove the English advance guard back across the stream they had been crossing. This small sign of Bruce's valor become a symbol of the war itself to the Scottish army, while Edward's soldiers were well-armed and imposing against the Scot's lightly armed but highly active forces. When Bruce was reproached by some of his men for the way he risked himself, he is said to only have regretted breaking the handle of his axe. Henty goes on to say that Bruce:

"...assembled all his principal leaders round him, and after thanking God for so fair a beginning of the fight as had that day been made, he pointed out to them how great an effect the two preliminary skirmishes would have upon the spirits of both armies, and expressed his confidence in the final result. He urged upon them the necessity for keeping their followers well in hand, and meeting the charges of the enemy's horse steadily with their spears; and especially warned them, after repulsing a charge, against allowing their men to break their array, either to plunder or take prisoners, so long as the battle lasted, as the whole riches of the English camp would fall into their hands if successful. He pledged himself that the heirs of all who fell should have the succession of their estates free from the usual feudal burdens on such occasions.

On the next day, Monday, the two armies drew up to each other in preparation for battle. King Edward seeing the Scottish army pause and kneel for prayer, commented that they were praying for mercy. Sir Ingram de Umfraville is said to have replied "They ask for mercy, but not from you. They ask mercy of Heaven. Yon men will conquer, or die. None will flee for fear of death." This was an accurate summary of the Scottish moral at Bannockburn.

As the English approached, the Scottish archers began to shoot their arrows into the approaching English cavalry before the battle had "officially" begun. Angered at this, a number of the English charged before they were supposed to and were promptly cut down. From the English perspective, this started the battle prematurely, but it was a blessing for the Scots.

The Scots were extremely bold, standing in lines facing the charging horses of the English and taking turns rushing out with battle-axes and chopping at the mounted knights. This was important because once an armored soldier was brought to the ground, he was as good as dead. The very size and strength of the English army was working against the English. The English cavalry smashed into their own infantry and there was utter mayhem; they were tripping over their own casualties.

The Scots had dedicated their entire military force to this battle and were fighting like foxes in a corner. The English did have reserves, but could not access them with all of the confusion. With the English formations beginning to break, the Scots raised their war cries and continued shouting "Lay on! Lay on! They fail!" Bruce's camp followers heard the cry and quickly rushed on to the battle field to help the Scottish army. The English army, ready to flee, saw this as reinforcements appearing and completely lost their nerve. Edward fled with his personal bodyguard, and the British defeat turned into a strong Scottish victory. It is said that 11,000 English were killed, while the Scottish losses seemed to be light, having only two knights killed in the battle. John Joseph Lalor said:

> The generalship of Bruce and the bravery of his men inflicted on England, that day, a defeat and a humiliation greater than ever befell her in all her history before or since, with the exception of the battle of Hastings. Her mighty host became a very chaos. The confusion of their flight was irremediable. The booty obtained was very rich, and articles taken at Bannockburn were treasured as heirlooms for centuries. An immense sum was also acquired by the Scots as ransoms for their noble captives.

Although Scottish independence was not going to be recognized for another decade, the Battle of Bannockburn solidified the Scots. In the Scots' mind there could only be one ending to this struggle for Scotland: complete freedom from English oppression. Lalor also says:

> The battle of Bannockburn marks an important epoch in Scottish history. The patriotic feelings excited and the glory acquired on that day consolidated the nation as it had never been before. It engraved on the Scottish heart a pride of their independence as a nation, which for centuries prevented a union with England; and to this day, like Thermopylæ and Marathon, it fires many a heart with an enthusiasm for liberty.

THE DECLARATION OF ARBROATH

Decisive battles pave the way for fundamental cultural changes for either for good or evil. The Battle of Bannockburn did just that. It created the foundation for the necessary leverage needed for future leaders of Scotland to stand together in the formation of two very important principles.

These principles would be laid forth in a very important document, setting forth for the first time, in writing, the national identity and independence of the Scottish people. It was also to set forth before the world and before the Pope that all people and all kings are ultimately under God and that they may not act in a usurpative manner towards their people. This document was the Declaration of Arbroath.

Standing in the wake of Bannockburn, the Scottish nobles rose together and signed *The Declaration of Arbroath*. They begin by giving an apologetic, a defense for why they believe that it was not right for England and the Pope to be going after the Scots. Their reason: they believe that they are Christ's chosen people, witnessed to by the Apostle Andrew, evangelized by men like Columba. They write that "the King of kings and Lord of lords, our Lord Jesus Christ, after His Passion and Resurrection, called [the Scots], even though settled in the uttermost parts of the earth, almost the first to His most holy faith."

The Scots were saying that they were a special people who had been in

Scotland for a long time and who had fought off other invaders. They were also practically saying what right do you have, oh Pope, to stick your nose into our business? It is your job to defend us as a sacred people, not attack us! And if you continue to work against us and don't act in our defense, God will judge you! And we will never give up! That was the Scots' message!

After giving their history of how the nation came about and of their record of freedom for a thousand years, they go on to speak of how in the past the church had been their help. But now the Pope had actually been backing the English, both in word and deed! So the Scots list the atrocities of this King and his deeds "of cruelty, massacre, violence, pillage, arson, imprisoning prelates, burning down monasteries, robbing and killing monks and nuns, and yet other outrages without number which he committed against our people, sparing neither age nor sex, religion nor rank, no one could describe nor fully imagine unless he had seen them with his own eyes." It is very interesting to note the similarities we see in the Declaration of Arbroath to the United States Declaration of Independence, written almost five hundred years later. The United States Declaration of Independence begins with an appeal to God, and then goes on to speak of the outrages committed against the American people using the very same types of verbiage that the Scottish nobles had used. They both use this same type of measured, but strong language in response to tyranny.

The Scottish nobles go on to say that, though all this had happened, though they had been mistreated, God had raised up a defense for his people in the form of a "most tireless prince" Robert Bruce. (And though we have assented to Bruce as our king and leader, if he ever turns on us we'll take him out just like that!) All men must be under jurisdictions, even the "good" kings. We, as people of God, are no respecter of persons, we do not hold to a double standard, and we are completely free people under God! They then give the memorable words which have gone down in history as a declaration of freedom.

> *...for, as long as but a hundred of us remain alive, never will we on any conditions be brought under English rule. It is in truth not for glory, nor riches, nor honours that we are fighting, but for freedom —for that alone, which no honest man gives up but with life itself.*

They close the document by saying that now that they have explained the truth to the Pope, if he, and all other men, continue to ignore the Scots and back the antagonism of the English, then surely God will lay the blood of all the men killed upon the soul of the Pope, and any others who continue to act antagonistically towards them.

Today we can look to the Declaration of Arbroath as an inspiring document behind the charters and declarations of America's birth.

GROUP DISCUSSIONS AND QUESTIONS

1. Finish this sentence: Men follow _____.

2. What was William Wallace's personal grief against the English?

3. This personal grief represented what fundamental philosophical problem that Wallace had with England's role in Scotland?

4. What are the principles of leadership manifested in the life of William Wallace which prepared him for greatness.

5. Describe several "larger than life" aspects of William Wallace.

6. What is true about the cost paid by every great leader?

7. Why is Wallace and the Scottish War for Independence significant to the Scottish Reformation of the 16th century?

8. Why were the Knights of Templar founded?

9. How is the Battle at Stirling the equivalent of our Bunker Hill or Dorchester Heights?

10. What had the Scots learned from their defeat at Falkirk that led to a change of strategy in their military preparation under the leadership of Robert the Bruce which ultimately helped them win at Bannockburn?

11. How did Bruce pick up the mantle of Wallace?

12. What had been his ambivalence previously?

13. What kind of a leader was Edward II?

14. What was the impact of the Battle at Bannockburn?

15. To what great Greek battles is Bannockburn compared?

16. What are the critical points of the Declaration of Arbroath?

17. What are the similarities between this Declaration and our own Declaration of Independence?

LECTURES AND VIDEO SERIES

Audio: Wallace Monument, Stirling Castle, Bannockburn

Video: Day 11-Mine Warfare, Day 12-The Wallace Monument, Day 12-Stirling Castle, Day 12-Bannockburn, Day 12-Bannockburn Charge

FURTHER STUDY AND RECOMMENDED READING

In Freedom's Cause, by G.A. Henty

Both Sides of the Border, by G.A. Henty

Bannockburn, 1314: Robert Bruce's Great Victory, by Pete Armstrong

Stirling Bridge & Falkirk, 1297-98, by Pete Armstrong

Scottish Battlefields: 500 Battles that Shaped Scottish History, Tempus, 2008, by Chris Brown,

Life in a Medieval Village, by Frances and Joseph Gies

Life in a Medieval Castle, by Frances and Joseph Gies

The Battle of Bannockburn, 1314, by Aryeh Nusbacher

How the Scots Saved Christendom, by Vision Forum (CD)

CHAPTER XVI

THE SCOTTISH REFORMATION

We find that it has been the constant practice of the Lord's people in
all ages, to hand down and keep on record what the Lord had done
by and for their forefathers in former times.
—*John Howie,* The Scots Worthies

THE MARTYRS OF ST. ANDREWS

As the Reformation began to grow from Germany and Geneva into England and Scotland, the Roman Catholic church began to crack down on the rebels and heretics who dared to go against the papacy. It was during this time that the days of martyrdom and burning began around Europe. To believe in any of the *Solas* of the Reformation, or even in "Scriptures alone" as doctrine, was in enough to sentence a person to death.

The four martyrs of St. Andrews were Patrick Hamilton martyred in 1528, Henry Forrest in 1533, George Wishart in 1546, and Walter Myln in

1558. Each of these men were martyred for the beliefs that they had come to from relying on the Scriptures as their sole source of understanding.

Patrick Hamilton was only twenty-four years of age when he was martyred in the city of Saint Andrews. He had been a student teacher at the College of St. Andrew's College when on February 29, 1528, he was taken by Archbishop Beaton, tried for heresy, and burned at the stake in front of the very college in St. Andrews where he had taught.

The so-called heretical statements which he died for were that men should not pray to Mary, that they should not pray to the dead, and that the Bible is sufficient for faith and practice. These were the beliefs of the Reformation and these were the beliefs that this young man was willing to die for. He was brought before Archbishop Beaton who required him to recant these "heresies of the faith." When Hamilton refused, he was dragged out and brought into the square. The students and teachers did not believe that he was really going to be burned. They thought that he was being tested or that it was a joke. John Foxe says:

> When he arrived at the stake, he kneeled down, and, for some time prayed with great fervency. After this he was fastened to the stake, and the fagots placed round him. A quantity of gunpowder having been placed under his arms was first set on fire which scorched his left hand and one side of his face, but did no material injury, neither did it communicate with the fagots. In consequence of this, more powder and combustible matter were brought, which being set on fire took effect, and the fagots being kindled, he called out, with an audible voice: "Lord Jesus, receive my spirit! How long shall darkness overwhelm this realm? And how long wilt Thou suffer the tyranny of these men?"

The spectators called out for him to cry "Salve Regina" to which he replied, "Depart from me, and trouble me not, ye messengers of Satan." Patrick Hamilton died as a Christian martyr at age twenty-four. His last words were "Lord Jesus, receive my spirit." And as is so often the case, his death drew even more people to the Reformation because of his courageous bearing and testimony.

Five years later in 1533, a young Benedictine friar named Henry Forrest commented to another that he thought Hamilton a good man and that the beliefs he had died for might be defended. This was enough to sentence Forrest to death. John Lindsay, one of the Archbishop's men, recommended that Forrest be burned in a cellar because "the smoke of Patrick Hamilton hath infected all those on whom it blew." And so it was. Forrest died of the suffocating flames in that cellar.

Today, most men are not willing to defend the people they agree with. We live in a world of cowards. As Christians, we must respond by understanding that there is a price to pay for truth, and we must be willing to pay it. The Bible doesn't say the godly in Christ might suffer persecution, it says "Yea, and all that will live godly in Christ Jesus shall suffer persecution" (2 Timothy 3:12). Men who stand for truth inspire others to follow their example. Embrace difficulty, embrace persecution: God uses it to build character and to embolden others.

Because these young men were willing to give their lives in defense of what they believed, many others followed in their example and helped to stem the tide of Catholicism. We must be prepared to stand for things which are right. And we must not be scared of receiving the consequences. We must understand the consequences and face them. All of life is preparation for brief moments of opportunity where the light of the Gospel of Jesus Christ will shine bright through our examples. We need strong courageous Christians, and we need to understand that our fathers in the faith died to give us these opportunities.

SAMUEL RUTHERFORD

Epitaph of Samuel Rutherford:

What tongue, what pen, or skill of men
Can famous Rutherford commend!

His learning justly rais'd his fame
True goodness did adorn his name.

He did converse with things above,
Acquainted with Immanuel's love.

Most orthodox he was and sound,
And many errors did confound.

For Zion's King, and Zion's cause,
And Scotland's covenanted laws,

Most constantly he did contend,
Until his time was at an end.

At last he won to full fruition
Of that which he had seen in vision.

In 1776, one of the best-sellers was a book written by a Calvinist. This book, *Lex Rex*, or *The Law As King*, was one of the most important influences on the American War for Independence. Written as a response to "Rex Lex", the belief that the king is the law, this important work deals with a proper theory of limited government and placed the government in a position as under the law.

Samuel Rutherford, author of *Lex Rex*, was born at the turn of the 17th century, shortly after the second wave of the Reformation which had been led by men like John Calvin and John Knox. It was in 1625, during the beginning of Rutherford's ministry, that King Charles I came to the throne of England. Charles was a strong advocate of the theory that the king was law, and he also hated the "non-comformists" and Puritans. This jurisdictional contest between Charles' rights and Parliament's rights escalated into the English Civil War. Charles only worsened his political and constitutional position by bringing in foreign mercenaries to "put down" his own people in England.

Parliament, in an effort to unite the turmoil torn people of England, decided to circumvent economics and politics and attempt to unite the people religiously by creating a document which would be a "confession of faith" to the rest of the world.

Parliament also needed to defend itself against the physical attacks being made by Charles, and so turned to Presbyterian and reformed Scotland, asking them to send troops to help. Scotland saw an opportunity and proposed a "solemn league and covenant." If Parliament would covenant with God and man to defend the Reformed faith in its worship, doctrine, practice, and government, then Scotland would give military assistance. Parliament also had to swear to work toward the reformation of the Church of England in discipline, worship, organization, and theology.

Parliament agreed and gathered the needed representatives to work out the details of the statement of faith. In 1643, the Westminster Assembly was convened and Samuel Rutherford was one of five Scottish commissioners invited to participate. One hundred and twenty men came together to produced the Westminster Confession of Faith and Catechisms. The later London Baptist Confession of Faith was based almost exclusively on the Westminster Confession. While the five Scots serving as commissioners, Samuel Rutherford, George Gillespie, Alexander Henderson, and Earl Worleston did not have direct authority in the assembly, they by far had a dominant influence.

One of the great differences between the Scottish Reformation and the English Reformation was that the English Reformation's emphasis was on the rights and liberties of free Englishmen. The emphasis in Scotland was on the rights and prerogatives of King Jesus, the head of the Church. This is why the Rutherford and the Scots always wrote about "Zion's Call".

It was during this time that Rutherford wrote *Lex Rex, The Law as King*. Later this book would be brought to America and would lay the foundation for the American understanding of Romans 13 and a proper understanding of resistance of tyranny.

Of the letters of Samuel Rutherford, Spurgeon would later write, "When we are dead and gone, let the world know that Spurgeon held Rutherford's letters to be the nearest thing to inspiration which can be found in all the writings of mere men." This is the sort of man Samuel Rutherford was considered to be by the "prince of preachers" himself!

At the end of his life, Rutherford was summoned to come to the king to give an account of his "treasonous" teachings. Rutherford knew what was awaiting him when he would come to meet the king, almost certain death, but he also knew something the king didn't. When the soldiers came to summons him to the king, Rutherford was on his deathbed and only responded to the soldiers that he had " a summons already before a superior judge and judicatory, and I behoove to answer my first summons, and ere your day come I will be where few kings and great folks come."

What a proper way for the man who had defended God over kings to go out! And how providential it is that in the same city, St. Andrews, where men like Wishart and Hamilton gave their lives in defense of the word of God, Samuel Rutherford should be buried. Rutherford was another of the important reformers of Scotland and a man who helped to give the theology behind the birth of America.

JOHN KNOX AND THE THE COVENANTERS

One of the most important men to influence the Reformation at large, and not only the Reformation in Scotland, was John Knox. Alongside Calvin, Knox would help to clearly define and defend the doctrines of Reformation in an era when to do so often meant death. No man had as great an impact on any individual country as John Knox did on Scotland. Through Scotland, many other men and nations were enabled to move into the dawn of Reformation.

Toward the end of the Middle Ages, the Reformation was birthed by men like Wycliffe. But the very beginning of the reformation can really be traced to October 31, 1517, when Martin Luther, a young Augustinian monk, nailed his 95 Theses of controversies to the doors of the Wittenberg Church. He had written his theses in Latin, but during the night, a publisher read them and translated them into German so that they could be published. The next day it spread like wild fire.

One of the many men influenced by Luther was a young man named George Wishart. Wishart, in turn, began to influence a young man named John Knox in the middle fifteen hundreds. Knox as a young convert would follow Wishart around with a broadsword, because Wishart, being at war with the Roman church, was in constant peril. One day Wishart was called to St. Andrews, and he knew that he was going to be killed when he got there. Knox, ready to go as his defender, was told by Wishart to stay behind because one sacrifice for the Lord was sufficient. Wishart was burned at the stake in front of Cardinal Beaton on March 1, 1546. Because of his Wishart's foresight, Knox was spared to become Scotland's greatest preacher.

On June 29, 1547, a fleet of French galley ships approached St. Andrews, where Knox had been preaching, and besieged the castle. The garrison surrendered on July 31st, most the men of the castle, including Knox, were taken and made to row in the French galleys where they were chained to benches, whipped and made to row all day as slaves. John Knox as a stubborn Scot and never gave in to the prodding of the French Catholic crew. Once the crew tried to force Knox to show devotion to a picture of the Virgin Mary, he was told to kiss the idol in veneration. When he refused, it was pushed up to his face. He seized it and threw it into the sea, saying, "Let our Lady now save herself: she is light enough: let her learn to swim." It is during this time of imprisonment that Knox vowed to return to St. Andrews and preach again, saying, "I am fully persuaded, how weak so ever I now appear, I shall not depart this life till my tongue shall glorify His Holy Name in the same place." Sometime in February of 1549, Knox was released after serving roughly nineteen months as a galley slave.

Having gained his freedom, Knox continued to heartily participate in the reformation in both England and Scotland. He helped Bishop Cranmer, who was serving under Henry VIII, to subversively spread the Reformation doctrines in England by supplying ignorant Catholic priests with reformation sermons which they were required, by the King, to preach every Sunday. When Henry VIII died, Knox became the chaplain to the teenage King Edward VI, and the Reformation accelerated. Edward died, and Jane Grey was killed after nine days, and Mary Tudor, daughter of Henry VIII and Catherine of Aragon, whose goal it was to unravel the Reformation, came to power. Three hundred people were tortured and burned at the stake under Mary, including Cranmer. Knox did not want to flee, but was finally convinced by his friends to leave. After a short time in Frankfurt, Germany, he left for Geneva, studied under Calvin, and helped to write the Geneva Bible. In 1559 he returned to Scotland and continued to preach throughout the country in church after church. And so, Scotland was reformed by the Word of God when England was still just beginning to learn. Knox's preaching was so powerful that the peasants destroyed the Roman church at St. Andrews when they fully understood the danger of Catholicism. Knox said:

> [L]ively faith makes men bold, and is able to carry us through such perils as are inescapable to nature. But when faith begins to faint, then man begins to sink down in every danger. . . .

Thomas M'Crie in his *Life of John Knox* says:

> Spare no arrows," was the motto which Knox wore on his standard; the authority of Scripture, and the force of reasoning, grave reproof, and pointed irony, were in their turn employed by him. In the course of this defense, he did not restrain those sallies of raillery, which the fooleries of the popish superstition irresistibly provoke, even from those who are deeply impressed with its pernicious tendency.

During one of Knox's confrontations with Mary, Queen of Scots, she accused him of turning her subjects against her through his book *The First Blast of the Trumpet Against the Monstrous Regiment of Women.* Knox answered her boldly:

> ...if to teach the Truth of God in sincerity, if to rebuke Idolatry and to will a people to worship God according to His Word, be to raise subjects against their Princes, then can I not be excused; for it hath pleased God of His Mercy to make me one among many to disclose unto this Realm the vanity of the Papistical Religion, and the deceit, pride, and tyranny of that Roman Antichrist. But, Madam, if the true knowledge of God and His right worshipping be the chief causes, that must move men from their heart to obey their just Princes, as it is most certain they are, wherein can I be reprehended? I am surely persuaded that Your Grace has had and presently has, as unfeigned obedience of such as profess Jesus Christ within this Realm, as ever your father or other progenitors had of those that were called Bishops.

And touching that Book which seemeth so highly to offend Your Majesty, it is most certain that I wrote it, and I am content that all the learned of the world judge of it. I hear that an Englishman hath written against it, but I have not read him. If he hath sufficiently [dis]proved my reasons, and established his contrary propositions with as evident testimonies as I have done mine, I shall not be obstinate, but shall confess my error and ignorance. But this hour I have thought, and yet think, myself alone to be more able to sustain the things affirmed in my work, than any ten in Europe shall be able to confute it.

Knox also spoke of the people's duty to resist tyranny of governance and stated, to Mary's face, that:

"...[if] princes exceed their bounds, Madam, no doubt they may be resisted, even by power. For there is no greater honour, nor greater obedience, to be given to kings or princes, than God hath commanded to be given unto father and mother. But the father may be stricken with a frenzy, in which he would slay his children. If the children arise, join themselves together, apprehend the father, take the sword from him, bind his hands, and keep him in prison till his frenzy be overpast—think ye, Madam, with princes that would murder the children of God that are subjects unto them. Their blind zeal is nothing but a very mad frenzy, and therefore, to take the sword from them, to bind their hands, and to cast them into prison, till they be brought to a sober mind, is no disobedience against princes, but just obedience, because it agreeth with the will of God."

The queen was so stunned at these words that she sat for "more than the quarter of an hour - her countenance altered." Finally she responded to Knox:

"Well then, I perceive that my subjects shall obey you, and not me. They shall do what they list, and not what I command; and so I must be subject to them, and not they to me."

The dialogue continued, and at the conclusion of the conversation Knox, as a Christian gentleman stated, "I pray God, Madam, that ye may be as blessed within the Commonwealth of Scotland, if it be the pleasure of God, as ever Deborah was in the Commonwealth of Israel."

Knox continued to serve as the leader of the Scottish Reformation throughout Mary's reign. Throughout his life, Knox taught the doctrine of the Regulative principle of worship and the doctrine of the Providence of God. He was the primary influence on the Christian growth of Scotland in the sixteenth century.

Sadly, today John Knox is all but forgotten by the Scottish people and is buried under parking lot number 23 with no plaque and only a small brass marker which does not even give his name. This is truly a tragedy of dishonor and ingratitude. There are church buildings and monuments everywhere, but few of them even mention Knox or his influence on Christianity. When we forget to honor our fathers and mothers, we build a culture of ingratitude and we lose the past. We must remember and we must tell the stories in the spirit of Psalm 78, to inspire a generational vision, so that our sons and daughters will be mighty in the land and honor God until Christ's return.

> *Give ear, O my people, to my law: incline your ears to the words of my mouth. 2 I will open my mouth in a parable: I will utter dark sayings of old: 3 Which we have heard and known, and our fathers have told us. 4 We will not hide them from their children, shewing to the generation to come the praises of the LORD, and his strength, and his wonderful works that he hath done. 5 For he established a testimony in Jacob, and appointed a law in Israel, which he commanded our fathers, that they should make them known to their children: 6 That the generation to come might know them, even the children which should be born; who should arise and declare them to their children: 7 That they might set their hope in God, and not forget the works of God, but keep his commandments. —Psalm 78:1-7*

Exodus 20:12 says, "Honour thy father and thy mother: that thy days may be long upon the land which the LORD thy God giveth thee." We will not benefit from the Fifth Commandment if we forget or are ungrateful to our fathers in the Lord. John Knox, in large part has been forgotten. May the legacy of John Knox be revived so that men may know about Knox's great and mighty God.

In the Scottish Confession of Faith, 1560 Knox said:

> We confess and believe all things in heaven and in earth to be
> ruled and guided by His inscrutable providence to such ends as His
> eternal wisdom, goodness, and justice has appointed them to the
> manifestation of His own glory.

Knox was a man who understood that God directs in all things. This is what gives the Christian hope. It is through difficulty, persecution, and perseverance that God forges His church and puts out his sustaining hand of grace to bless the Christian and give him hope. Without hope nations cannot be built, marriages cannot be founded on the right foundation, but as Christians we have true hope in Christ and his providence. Knox said:

> Stand with Christ in this day of his battle, which shall be short
> and the victory everlasting! For the Lord himself shall come in our
> defense with his mighty power; He shall give us the victory when the
> battle is most strong. . . .

May we honor the memory of the men who helped to build up the faith, found our nation, and inspire generations. If we do so, we will be able to have true hope in the providence of God! The gates of hell shall never prevail against the church of the Lord Jesus Christ!

THE KILLING TIMES AND THE LEGACY OF GREYFRIARS KIRKYARD

Our great journey through 2,000 years of Western Civilization now approaches its end as we enter the poignant and powerful location of Greyfriars Kirkyard.

The Covenanters, whose beliefs were founded on Reformers like John Knox, reached their supreme testing point in the 1680s. It was during this season that many of the Scot Presbyterians, some of whom had even supported the restoration of Charles II, would face the ultimate test in their belief as to whether or not Christ was the true and only head of the church.

The Killing Times marked a dark season in Scottish history that took place in response to the rise of the Scottish Covenanter movement. Between the time period of Charles II and James VII, the Scots committed to the authority of Christ over the Church, and rose in opposition to the hegemony of the English monarch to dominate that which belonged exclusively to Christ. They refused to submit to the acts of supremacy that were being foisted upon them. Meeting in glens and private conventicles they continued to preach the word of God. But British troops entered into Scotland, found them out, harried them out of the country in some cases, and in other cases forced them to either submit or to be executed.

Perhaps no place in the city of Edinburgh is as poignant and meaningful to the history of the church of Jesus Christ as Greyfriars Kirkyard. It was in Greyfriars Kirkyard that on February 28, 1638, the preachers of Scotland came together and drafted the Scottish National Covenant. This document rejected the attempt by King Charles I and Archbishop Laud to force the Scottish church to conform to English liturgical practice and church governance. The covenant reaffirmed Reformed faith and presbyterian form of worship and denounced the attempted changes, but it also urged loyalty to the king.

Forty years later, it would also be in Greyfriars Kirkyard that several thousand faithful men, women, and children of the Covenanters were rounded up and imprisoned to starve, rot, and die. This was for refusing to submit to the unlawful and unbiblical decrees of the King which had been rejected when he demanded supremacy over the Church.

The names of men and women like Richard Cameron, Margaret Wilson, John Brown, and many others, became famous among the lists of Scottish martyrs, because they were among the first to give up their lives rather than deny the supremacy of Jesus Christ of his Church itself. In the end, tens of thousands of men, women, and children would be put to death in horrific ways before the season of the killing times came to an end. A glorious monument to those who died and all the Covenanters is now in the graveyard of Greyfriars Kirk. The monument has memorialized in stone the tremendous sacrifice of the covenanters and their legacy.

The history of Scotland, which traces the remarkable legacies of men set apart in their passion for freedom, liberty, and independence, truly found its high point and zenith in the Christian witness and testimony and legacy of the Scottish Covenanters throughout the 16th and 17th centuries.

What in fact really was the legacy left by these men? It was a legacy of truly understanding the proper relationship between the Church and the State. It was legacy of fighting for the fundamentals of the faith. It was a legacy of seeing that true freedom comes from the law of God. And all of these legacies were exported to the United States of America where they took root in the soil of freedom and ultimately emerged into documents like the Declaration of Independence.

The story of the martyrs of the Killing Times is, in a very real sense, the story of the people of the United States, because it was the offspring of the martyrs, the sons, the daughters, the children who survived, who would go on to write the books, some of whom would come to the United States of America, and pass on that spirit liberty and freedom to a new people, a free people.

Thus we begin to see just how central Greyfriars Kirkyard is to the story of the Covenanters and to the story of Christianity throughout the world.

THE MARTYRS' MONUMENT

Halt passenger, take heed what you do see,
This tomb doth shew for what some men did die.

Here lies interr'd the dust of those who stood
'Gainst perjury, resisting unto blood;

Adhering to the Covenants, and laws

Establishing the same, which was the Cause

Then their lives were sacrific'd unto the lust
Or Prelatist's abjur'd. Though here their dust

Lies mixt with murderers, and other crew
Whom justice justly did to death pursue:

But as for them, no cause was found
Worthy of death, but only they were found,

Constant and steadfast, zealous, witnessing,
For the Prerogatives of CHRIST their KING,

Which Truths were seal'd by famous Guthrie's head
And all along to Mr Renwick's blood.

They did endure the wrath of enemies,
Reproaches, torments, deaths and injuries

But yet they're those who from such troubles came,
And now triumph in glory with the LAMB.

*From May 27th 1661 that the most noble Marquis of Argyle was beheaded, to
the 17th of Feb'ry 1688 that Mr. James Renwick suffered; were one way or other
Murdered and Destroyed for the same Cause, about Eighteen thousand of whom were
execute[d] at Edinburgh, about an hundred of Noblemen Gentlemen, Ministers and
Others noble Martyrs for JESUS CHRIST. The most of them lies here.*

*For a particular account of the cause and manor of their suffering see The Cloud of
Witnesses, Crookshank's and Defoe's Histories.*

GROUP DISCUSSIONS AND QUESTIONS

1. Connect the historical dots from Samuel Rutherford to the forming of
   these United States.

2. Using George Wishart and John Knox as examples, explain the power of
   friendship and discipleship.

3. What are the three points of the *Lex Rex*, as given by Dr. Morecraft. Talk about them. Do you agree with them? How should we implement them today?

4. Explain how the Cathedral at St. Andrews was destroyed.

5. List the charges for which Patrick Hamilton was burned at the stake.

6. Name the charge for which Henry Forrest was burned at the stake. What is different about the way in which Forrest was martyred? What is significant about this?

7. What is the name of the Roman Catholic prelate from St. Andrews who persecuted the reformers and was ultimately murdered?

8. What is the lesson for us today from the lives of Patrick Hamilton, Henry Forrest, and Walter Myln?

9. What is the key to restoring unity in a kingdom? Hint: it is not political.

10. Name the three main points of the *Lex Rex* written by Samuel Rutherford in 1643. Why was this so important during our nation's struggle for independence one hundred years later?

11. What was the mining/counter-mining incident that took place underneath St. Andrews castle at the time that the reformers were holed up there?

12. Define these architectural terms: broch, keep, crows nest, gables, angle turret.

13. What is the name of the traditional style of architecture used by the Scots in the 18th and 19th centuries after the classical and Renaissance period?

14. Summarize the Solemn League and Covenant.

15. Finish the sentence: "The blood of the martyrs is the. . ." Why is this true?

16. The two great flaws of Medieval Scholasticism are as follows: 1) It attempted to explain the doctrines of Christianity within the structures of Greek and Roman philosophy. 2) It rejected the total depravity of man and gave man credit in the salvation process, creating a religion of merit, a system whereby man cooperates with God's grace for his own salvation.

17. Where do we see these same flaws today in the church?

18. Finish the sentence: "Medieval scholasticism offered the world a savior who would help men save themselves; the Reformation doctrines offered the world a Savior who would. . ."

19. What was James Guthrie's exhortation to his son? What was the long term result of that exhortation?

20. Who is buried in Greyfriars Kirkyard?

21. What were the Killing Times?

LECTURES AND VIDEO SERIES

Audio: St. Andrews, John Knox 1, John Knox 2, Greyfriars Kirkyard: Chronology Hamilton to the Covenanters, 2000 Years Perseverance and the Church of Jesus Christ, Doctrines of the Apostles

Video: Day 11-Welcome to St. Andrews, Day 11-Lex Rex, Day 11-Young Martyrs, Day 11-The Rise of Knox, Day 11-St. Andrews Castle, Day 11-St. Andrews Castle, Part 2, Day 11-St. Andrews Wrap-Up, Day 13-St. Giles, Day 13-Parking Space 23, Day 13-The Killing Times, Day 13-Greyfriars Kirkyard, Day 13-Wrap-Up, Q&A Final Session, Closing Ceremonies

FURTHER STUDY AND RECOMMENDED READING

The Letters of Samuel Rutherford

Westminster Confession of Faith

A Scottish Christian Heritage, by Iain Murray

Fair Sunshine, by Jock Purves

The Scots Worthies, by John Howie

Family Reformation, by Scott Brown

The Reformation: A Handbook, by T.M. Lindsay

History of the Reformation in Europe in the Time of Calvin, by Merle D'Aubigne

Foxe's Book of Martyrs, by John Foxe

The Scots Worthies, by John Howie

Scottish Covenanter Stories: Tales from the Killing Times, by Dane Love

Life of John Knox, by Thomas McCrie

The Story of the Scottish Church, by Thomas McCrie

A Cloud of Witnesses, For the Royal Prerogatives of Jesus Christ, by John H. Thomson

How the Scots Saved Christendom, by Vision Forum (CD)

Stories of the Covenanters in Scotland, by Robert Pollok

Reformation Heroes, by Diana Kleyn and Joel Beeke

History of the Reformation In the 16th Century, by Merle D'Aubigne

Famous Women of the Reformed Church, by James I. Good

Hunted and Harried, by R.M. Ballantyne

The Crown and Covenant Collection, by Douglas Bond

The Scottish Covenanters (DVD)

SCRIPTURE
MEMORIZATION

CHRISTIANITY AND ROME

Isaiah 46:9-11: "Remember the former things of old: for I am God, and there is none else; I am God, and there is none like me, Declaring the end from the beginning, and from ancient times the things that are not yet done, saying, My counsel shall stand, and I will do all my pleasure: Calling a ravenous bird from the east, the man that executeth my counsel from a far country: yea, I have spoken it, I will also bring it to pass; I have purposed it, I will also do it."

2 Corinthians 10:3-5: "For though we walk in the flesh, we do not war after the flesh: (For the weapons of our warfare are not carnal, but mighty through God to the pulling down of strong holds;) Casting down imaginations, and every high thing that exalteth itself against the knowledge of God, and bringing into captivity every thought to the obedience of Christ."

Ephesians 5:11: "And have no fellowship with the unfruitful works of darkness, but rather reprove them."

GENEVA AND FRANCE

Isaiah 62:1: "For Zion's sake will I not hold my peace, and for Jerusalem's sake I will not rest, until the righteousness thereof go forth as brightness, and the salvation thereof as a lamp that burneth."

Isaiah 58:12: "And they that shall be of thee shall build the old waste places: thou shalt raise up the foundations of many generations; and thou shalt be called, 'The repairer of the breach, The restorer of paths to dwell in.'"

Psalm 90:16-17: "Let thy work appear unto thy servants, and thy glory unto their children. And let the beauty of the LORD our God be upon us: and establish thou the work of our hands upon us; yea, the work of our hands establish thou it."

ENGLAND AND THE RISE OF CHRISTENDOM

Deuteronomy 4:5-6: "Behold, I have taught you statutes and judgments, even as the LORD my God commanded me, that ye should do so in the land whither ye go to possess it. Keep therefore and do them; for this is your wisdom and your understanding in the sight of the nations, which shall hear all these statutes, and say, 'Surely this great nation is a wise and understanding people.'"

Hebrews 12:1-3: "Wherefore seeing we also are compassed about with so great a cloud of witnesses, let us lay aside every weight, and the sin which doth so easily beset us, and let us run with patience the race that is set before us, Looking unto Jesus the author and finisher of our faith; who for the joy that was set before him endured the cross, despising the shame, and is set down at the right hand of the throne of God. For consider him that endured such contradiction of sinners against himself, lest ye be wearied and faint in your minds."

2 Timothy 2:2: "And the things that thou hast heard of me among many witnesses, the same commit thou to faithful men, who shall be able to teach others also."

SCOTLAND TO AMERICA

Acts 5:29: "Then Peter and the other apostles answered and said, 'We ought to obey God rather than men.'"

Daniel 11:32: "And such as do wickedly against the covenant shall he corrupt by flatteries: but the people that do know their God shall be strong, and do exploits."

Isaiah 6:16-18: "Bind up the testimony, seal the law among my disciples. And I will wait upon the LORD, that hideth his face from the house of Jacob, and I will look for him. Behold, I and the children whom the LORD hath given me are for signs and for wonders in Israel from the LORD of hosts, which dwelleth in mount Zion."

KEY DEFINITIONS

CHRISTIANITY AND ROME

Antiquity - Ancient times

Asphyxiate - To die or lose consciousness due to impaired normal breathing caused by gas or other noxious agents; to choke or suffocate

Autonomous - Independent of all government; having the right to self-rule; subject to no laws other than those imposed by one's own self or agency

Civilization - A human culture or society, specifically one that has reached an advanced state of refinement in manners, art, laws, and customs and has rejected the grossness of savage life

Empire - A group of nations or peoples ruled by an emperor, an empress, or other powerful sovereign of government; usually a territory larger than a kingdom, as the former Babylonian Empire, Roman Empire, Byzantine Empire, etc.

Epistle - A letter, especially a formal one, such as the Apostolic epistles contained in the New Testament

Externalize - To make external; to embody in an outward form

Fate - The universal principle or ultimate agency by which the order of things is determined. In contrast to Divine Providence, which represents God's careful governance over creation, Fate stresses the irrationality and impersonal character of events that occur.

Idolatry - The worship of idols, images, or anything made with hands; the worship of any being other than the One True God

Inerrant - Without error

Infallible - Not fallible; absolutely trustworthy or sure; exempt from error

Mythology - A system of fables or fabulous opinions and doctrines respecting the deities which heathen nations have supposed to preside over the world or influence the affairs of it

Pagan - (Noun) a heathen; a Gentile, an idolater; any one who worships a false god; (Adjective) pertaining to or representative of the lifestyle or worldview of a pagan

Philosophy - The rational investigation of the truths and principles of being, knowledge, and conduct; one's theory of philosophy (how being, knowledge and ethics are to be understood) can be right or wrong, depending on their core assumptions

Polytheism - The doctrine of or belief in more than one god or many gods

Presupposition - A pre-theoretical assumption; a core and foundational principle that is assumed as the predicate for any further thought or discussion in a particular realm of ideas

Providence - The care and superintendence which God exercises over all His creation and creatures in governing them

Sovereign - Supreme in power; possessing ultimate and final authority

Statism - The principle of policy of concentrating extensive economic, political and related controls in the state at the expense of individual liberty

Syncretism - The attempted reconciliation or union of different or opposing principles, practices, or parties, as in philosophy or religion

Theology - The field or branch of study that examines God, His attributes, His relation to the universe, and how His character and purpose relates to the rest of the world

GENEVA AND FRANCE

Canton - A small territorial district which is a distinct state with its own independent government

Capricious - Subject to, or led by, caprice or whim; apt to change from opinions suddenly or to depart from one's purpose; fickle; unsteady; erratic

Colonization - The act of planting or establishing a colony by settling people in a particular region, often remote, for the purpose of cultivation, commerce and defense, and for permanent residence

Conciliation - An agreement to be reconciled, often after a state of hostilities has ensued

Divine Right of Kings - A political doctrine of royal absolutism that asserts that a monarch is subject to no earthly authority or accountability, deriving his right to rule directly from the will of God

Ecclesiastical - Of or pertaining to the church

Enlightenment - A philosophical movement of the 18th Century which championed the power of human reason above God's revelation, leading to fundamental changes in political, religious, and educational doctrine and practices across Europe's and later America's cultural landscape.

Exegesis - The manner in which one goes about explaining and interpreting the meaning of a specific text, particularly the Bible. Whenever one follows good principles of exegesis, the result is a correct interpretation of the text; whereas when bad principles are used, the wrong interpretation follows.

Huguenot - The term Huguenot, a variation of the Swiss Eidgenossen (meaning "Oath Comrades") was used beginning in the middle 16th Century to describe French Protestants who resisted the Catholic leadership in France and who sought to live and worship as Reformed Christians

Humanism - A view of theory and practice that elevates human reason and scientific inquiry above God, emphasizing human fulfillment in the natural world, all the while rejecting the importance of the belief in God and adherence to His Word as the standard for faith and practice

Inherent - A permanent and inseparable element, quality, or attribute existing in someone or some thing

Licentiousness - The state of being unrestrained by law or order; lascivious; lewd; immoral

Mentor - A trusted and influential counselor or teacher

Orthodox - Of or pertaining to conformance to the true doctrines of the Christian faith

Piety - Piety, in principle, is a compound of reverence of Almighty God and love of His character; piety, in practice, is the exercise of those affections in obedience to His will and devotion to His service

Prerogative - An exclusive right or privilege exercised by virtue of rank, right, privilege, etc.

Protestant - A name used of those who oppose the Roman Catholic Church and its doctrine and adhere to a Reformed or Evangelical view of Christianity; those who opposed Rome during the Reformation were first called Protestants

Reformation - The broad movement in the 16th Century to reject the corruption of religion advanced by the Roman Catholic Church and to return to the pure teaching of Scriptures that the Apostolic Fathers established. While the seeds of this movement were sown beforehand, Martin Luther's nailing of the Ninety-Five Theses on the door of the chapel in Wittenberg, Germany, on October 31, 1517 is commonly identified as the beginning of the Reformation

Refugee - A person who flees for refuge or safety, often to a foreign country, as in time of political upheaval, war, etc.

Revolution - (1) An overthrow or repudiation of an established civil, political, or religious system by the people governed; (2) a radical and pervasive change in society and the social structure, often made suddenly and sometimes accompanied by violence

Superstition - A belief or notion, not based on credible reason or knowledge, in or of the significance of a particular thing, circumstance, or occurrence, which often leads to an irrational fear of what is unknown or mysterious

Tyrannical - Despotic, as characteristic of a tyrant; unjustly cruel, harsh, arbitrary, or oppressive in the wielding of authority

ENGLAND AND THE RISE OF CHRISTENDOM

Archaeology - The study of historic peoples and their cultures by analysis of their artifacts, inscriptions, monuments, and other such remains, especially those that have been excavated

Artifact - An item such as a tool, or the remains of one, as a shard of pottery, characteristic of an earlier time or culture, especially one found at an archaeological excavation

Barbarian - One belonging to a savage, uncivilized culture whose manners and laws are characterized by brutality and rude behavior

Cathedral - The principle church of a diocese, containing the bishop's throne. Cathedrals have often been built over hundreds of years with great ornamentation and have generally been among the most substantial architectural achievements in a particular city or region

Chronology -The sequential order in which past events occurred; an established understanding of the order and timing of past events

Codification - (1) The act, process, or result of instituting particular rules and principles into a formal, binding code in order to govern a specific jurisdiction; (2) the reducing of unwritten customs or case law into statutory form

Dissenter - The name given to English Protestants who dissented from the Church of England during the 17th Century

Disseminate - To scatter or spread widely, as through sowing seed; to broadcast or disperse

Epic - Of unusually great size or extent; the term can be used to refer to pivotal events in history that shaped the world

Geometric - Resembling or employing the simple rectilinear or curvilinear lines or figures used in geometry. The term is used to describe painting, sculpture, architecture, and ornamentation of predominately geometric characteristics

Heretical - Unorthodox; at variance with accepted doctrine

Higher Criticism - A method of studying the Bible that rejects the authority of the Scriptures as a self-authenticating witness, and has as its object to test the validity of the Bible through evidences external to the Scriptures

Infrastructure - The basic underlying framework of a system or organization; often used in reference to the fundamental facilities and systems serving a country, city, or area

Martyr - A person who willingly suffers death rather than renounce their religious convictions

Reconnaissance - The act of reconnoitering, i.e., to inspect, observe, or survey an area or region (often an enemy or the enemy's camp) in order to gain useful information for military, engineering, geological, or other purposes.

Repository - A place where things are deposited and held, often in safekeeping

Socialistic - Of or pertaining to socialism, a theory or system of social organization that advocates the vesting of ownership and the means of production and distribution of capital, land, etc., in the community as a whole

Tinker - A mender of pots, kettles, and pans, etc., usually an itinerant

Vindication - (1) The state or act of being cleared from wrongful accusation, imputation, or suspicion; (2) to uphold or justify by argument or evidence

SCOTLAND TO AMERICA

Allegiance - Loyalty or devotion to a particular person, group, nation, or cause

Circumvent - To go around or bypass

Constitutional - (1) of or pertaining to the constitution of a state or organization; (2) In accordance with the provisions of an established constitution

Corroborate - To strengthen or make more certain; to confirm. Often said of evidence brought forward from one source or witness that agrees with that of another

Convoy - Any group of military vehicles traveling together under the same orders

Covenanter - A Scotsman during the 1600s who, by solemn oath, pledged to uphold a presbyterian form of church government as well as purity and simplicity of worship, rather than consent to an unbiblical church hierarchy and the unbiblical worship practices demanded of them by such tyrants as Charles I, Charles II and James VII of England; those who vowed to uphold either or both the National Covenant or the Solemn League and Covenant

Epitaph - A commemorative inscription (often written in poem form) on a tomb or mortuary monument about the person buried at that site

Hegemony - Leadership or predominant influence exercised by one group or individuals over others

Legend - A non-historical or unverifiable story handed down by tradition from earlier times and often accepted as true

Liturgical - Of or pertaining to the ceremonies, rituals, or practices that are part of formal public worship

Memorialize - To present a memorial to—either in word, stone or otherwise—in order to preserve the memory of a specific person or event

Non-Conformist - One who refuses to conform to the rites and mode of worship of an established church

Oppression - The exercise of authority or power in a burdensome, cruel, unreasonable, or unjust manner. The state of being oppressed

Promulgate - To make known by open declaration; publish; to proclaim formerly or put in operation (a law, decree of court, etc.)

Romanize - To make Roman in character; used either in reference to the culture and principles of the Roman Empire or the Roman Catholic Church

Papacy - The office or jurisdiction of the pope; the system of ecclesiastical government over which the pope claims to be the supreme head

The Regulative Principle of Worship - This doctrine is summarized by three propositions meant to govern formal worship: (1) Whatever is commanded is required; (2) Whatever is forbidden is prohibited; (3) Whatever is not commanded is forbidden

Summons - A command, message, or signal to appear at a specified place, usually before an established or self-proclaimed authority

Synonymous - Equivalent in meaning; expressing or implying the same idea

Tidings - News, information, or intelligence; an account of what has taken place

TEST AND QUIZ QUESTIONS FOR TEACHER/PARENT USE

ROME AND THE EARLY CHURCH

1. Who are believed to have been the founders of Rome?

2. Under which Caesars was the Colosseum of Rome built?

3. Name three types of events that took place in the Colosseum.

4. What enormous structure once existed right outside the location of the Colosseum, and was placed to honor a Roman Caesar?

5. Who were the first twelve Caesars of Rome?

6. How did the Romans borrow from the Greeks?

7. For what doctrine did Christians become the enemy of Rome?

8. How did the practices of the early Christians—represented by those who lived in the catacombs—differ from the practices and teachings of the later Roman Catholic Church?

9. Who guarded the Roman Caesar?

10. Name three classical Orders (architectural styles) that we observed that were used in Rome.

11. Which of the three main Architectural Orders is the largest/most favored by the Romans?

12. What is the name of the famous dome building built by Hadrian?

13. What was the other city that was wiped out by Mount Vesuvius?

GENEVA

1. Name two men, aside from John Calvin, who can be found on the Reformation Monument in Geneva.

2. What is the name of the small church building where Calvin trained his men and where Knox taught?

3. Who is responsible for provoking Calvin to stay in Geneva?

4. Name three ways that the doctrines of Calvin influenced the American view of government and freedom.

FRANCE

1. On what day and year was Charlemagne crowned emperor?

2. In Paris we saw an amazing iron tower. Who designed it?

3. Name one philosopher of the French Revolution.

4. When was 80% of Noyon destroyed?

5. What style of art, which makes use of naked cherubs, is represented at Versailles?

6. Name a great military officer and Reformer who was murdered in the anti-protestant massacres of France.

7. What was the name of the massacre?

8. Name three distinguishing aspects of Gothic architecture.

LONDON

1. Name two men buried in Bunhill Cemetery.

2. Name two pre-twentieth-century pastors of what is now called The Metropolitan Tabernacle.

3. Give the names of two artifacts from the British Museum which provide further testimony of the accuracy of the Bible.

4. Give two reasons why archaeology is important to the work of Reformation.

5. What ancient nation left the artifacts of lion hunting which are preserved at the British Royal Museum?

MIDDLE ENGLAND

1. Name three great Reformers entertained by Lady Willoughby at her castle.

2. What was the name of Catherine Willoughby's famous son, what does that name mean and, under what circumstance did he receive that name?

3. The classical front of Grimsthorpe castle was designed by whom?

4. What American founding father was inspired and trained by the Lord of Willoughby?

5. Name the famous poet, the puritan preacher, the printer, and the puritan political statesman whose lives intersected with Boston, England.

6. Who was the first great pastor of the future pilgrims from Scrooby?

7. Name the two most famous members of the pilgrim congregation.

YORK

1. Who did the Romans conquer pursuant to establishing York?

2. Who was crowned emperor in York, and why did he choose York?

3. Name four people groups that conquered and inhabited York.

4. Why is the famous street of York called the "shambles"?

5. What is the primary strategic concept behind siege warfare?

6. How long did it take to complete the minster? What does that tell you about multigenerational commitment to architectural and cultural objectives?

7. In what ways does the great cathedral of York evidence Roman Catholic syncretism?

ST. ANDREWS

1. What author wrote the most famous account of the four martyrs of St. Andrews?

2. Name two of the charges for which Patrick Hamilton was found guilty and condemned.

3. Who was the most famous student of George Wishart?

4. What stonework symbol commemorates the death of Hamilton and Wishart?

5. What wicked Roman Catholic prelate persecuted the Church in St. Andrews and was ultimately murdered?

6. What famous Reformer is buried near Samuel Rutherford?

7. Name the book that Rutherford penned in 1643 that influenced America's Founding Fathers?

WALLACE

1. Why are Wallace and the Scottish war for independence significant to the Reformation of the 16th century in Scotland?

2. Give two reasons why Wallace's victory at Stirling was important for the war for independence.

3. What is the significance of the Battle of Falkirk?

4. What English king fought at Bannockburn?

5. Who fought a great single combat the day before the great battle of Bannockburn?

6. What is the "baronial" style of architecture?

7. Give two reasons why the Declaration of Arbroath was important.

8. Why were the Knights Templar founded?

EDINBURGH AND THE COVENANTERS

1. Why were certain Scots described as Covenanters?

2. What was the motto of the Covenanters?

3. What was the defining issue for which the Covenanters fought?

4. Who was the "lion of the covenant"?

5. Where in Edinburgh were Covenanters executed?

6. According to the Martyrs Monument at the Greyfriars Cemetery, how many Covenanters were murdered during the "Killing Times"?

7. Name the first and last martyrs who were executed during the "Killing Times," as recorded on the Martyrs Monument at the Greyfriars Cemetery.

8. What is the parking lot number located behind St. Giles Kirk under which John Knox is buried?

GENERAL AND FOR EXTRA CREDIT

1. What is a providential view of history?

2. What is a biblical theory of architecture?

3. Give a brief chronology of Scottish Reformation history from the 1520s to the 1680s.

4. Offer an interpretation for the significance of the location of John Knox's grave.

5. Offer a one-paragraph Christian interpretation of the destruction of Pompeii.

6. In what ways did the Roman Catholic Church build on the foundation of Roman paganism?

7. Offer a brief description of the positive and negative influences of Constantine on Christianity and Western Civilization?

NOTES

NOTES